# A SMITH RIVER JOURNAL

## AN ADVENTURE OF FAITH, FATHERHOOD, & FRIENDSHIP

BRIAN G. MATTSON

SWINGING BRIDGE PRESS

ISBN-13: 978-0-9998723-2-1



Cover image: Polley, J. F, and Montana Railroad. *Map of central Montana, the Montana Railroad, September 1, 1899*. [N.P, 1899] Map. Retrieved from the Library of Congress, Control No: 98688722.



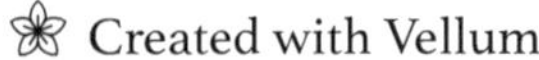

*For my shipmates,*
*Ty and Olivia,*
*And*
*The Boston Whaler Crew,*
*Bill and Betty*

# CONTENTS

*"The rivers of America are exceptionally beautiful. Everything is great and grand, graceful and noteworthy, it is all colossal. And there are beautiful views, beautiful beyond description."*

H. Bavinck, *My Journey to America*, 1892

*"The Smith is a postcard around every bend."*

Anonymous Rafter, 2017

# INTRODUCTION

My fourteen-year-old daughter Olivia and I are invited on an expedition. At least, we very much feel like Lewis and Clark in their "Voyage of Discovery." We are to float the Smith River in central Montana, a pristine wilderness canyon that stretches 59 miles from launch to take-out. Two hundred years ago Lewis and Clark themselves passed by the mouth of this tributary and named it the "Smith," after the Secretary of the Navy. Of course, they saw it as they were passing by *upstream* on the Missouri river. In those days, men were made differently. In those days there were men of renown.

It is mind-bending to think of the vast, complex network of waterways. More than once I marvel that the very water carrying us down a mountain canyon in remote Montana is water that will, in a few months' time, spill into the Gulf of Mexico. The Smith River begins in the Castle Mountains of Meagher County, fed by heavy snow melt. It flows between the Big Belt and Little Belt Mountains and winds its way northward toward Great Falls, Montana. There it meets up with the Missouri, the longest river in North America. It then journeys over two thousand miles and finally feeds the Big Muddy just north of Saint Louis. And then, like a lot of Montanans, it takes a trip to the Caribbean—"snowbird" water.

Access to the Smith River is tightly regulated. One may float by permit only, and permits are distributed through a random lottery. Each year 10,000 people apply, and only 1,000 permits are given. Many people try for decades before finally getting their chance. Our friend Ty Rosean hit this particular jackpot this year, and invites us to join him in his raft. Our total party at launch is 14 people in five vessels.

We are traveling through largely untouched wilderness—a river gorge with endless "S" curves; a deep cut in the crust of the earth, carved with what is at the same time the softest and the hardest known substance, that bonded molecular family of hydrogens and oxygen: water. It cleanses skin like silk; like diamond, it carves through rock. The same substance; a miracle of the first order, yet we hardly ever notice.

The same water that softly drifts us to our destination also carves the route through solid limestone and granite. The exposed layers of rock testify to the Ancient of Days —one cannot help but think of the phrase "foundations of the earth"—and cliff swallows who nest under its eaves by the thousands sing constant praise of his provision. Literally. They triumphantly sing as they dart, swoop, and flip just above the surface of the water, devouring the afternoon hatch just as the insects emerge from the depths to the surface.

As God's providence is evidenced by his provision for the swallows, it is also evident in the smallest details of our adventure. After decades now of studying high-octane theology, I have become increasingly convinced that one could actually summarize the whole of Christian faith under such headings as "Gift" and "Gratitude." The pagans neither "glorify God nor *give him thanks*," says Paul in his letter to the Romans. Sometimes the Christian life is as simple as that: being restored to a place where we can see the gifts, recognize them as gifts, and respond with true thankfulness. I see this more clearly in every meandering bend of the river.

---

"I am haunted by waters." So Norman MacLean ends his Pulitzer Prize winning novella, *A River Runs Through It*—the quintessential Montana memoir of hard men facing a harsh world. One cannot write or speak of rivers and Montana without reckoning with MacLean's moving and tragic tale. Waters are his metaphor for the elusive, unknowable movement of time, an ancient and uncontrollable power that masters mortal men. I am awed by waters, even unnerved by waters, but not haunted.

MacLean's opening paragraph is one of the best in all of literature:

> In our family, there was no clear line between religion and fly fishing. We lived at the junction of great trout rivers in western Montana, and our father was a Presbyterian minister and a fly fisherman who tied his own flies and taught others. He told us about Christ's disciples being fishermen, and we were left to assume, as my brother and I did, that all first-class fishermen on the Sea of Galilee were fly fishermen and that John, the favorite, was a dry-fly fisherman.

While I cannot "prove" my interpretation, I believe the key to the book—and its tragedy—is found in his next paragraph:

> In between on Sunday afternoons we had to study *The Westminster Shorter Catechism* for an hour and then recite before we could walk the hills with him while he unwound between services. But he never asked us more than the first question in the catechism, 'What is the chief end of man?' And we answered together so one of us could carry on if the other forgot, 'Man's chief end is to glorify God, and to enjoy Him forever.'

"So one of us could carry on if the other forgot." Norman and his brother Paul did forget, and neither was able to remind the other. The results were tragic. MacLean ends *A River Runs Through It* with poignant reflections on the "oneness" of all things, with the river and its waters symbolizing the flow of time with all its beauty and regret. He suggests that "telling stories" (as his father encouraged him to do) is a human way of imposing meaning upon that unknowable random flow—a kind of defiant projection on what is an ultimately inexplicable and chaotic world. He is haunted by waters because there is darkness in the depths.

But that catechism answer demands something different: all things are not one, but *two.* God and his creatures are distinct, and in a relationship that provides the latter a "chief end," a purpose, an ultimate meaning.

Our adventure on the river has a purpose, a goal. Waters do not haunt me because while the MacLean boys spoke with a rote memory that failed them, I recite but actually believe in the marrow of my bones the words of the *Westminster Shorter Catechism*. These reflections, this story, is one of glorifying and enjoying God in all his wonderful works; not only in the natural world, but in the personal world of the human: faith, fatherhood, and friendship.

# 1

# FAMILIAR & FOREIGN

"The Jews used to say that God had collected the dust for the human body from all the lands of the earth. Though the image is strange, a true and beautiful thought is expressed in it. As spirit, man is akin to the angels and soars to the invisible world; but he is at the same time a citizen of the visible world and connected with all physical creatures."

— H. Bavinck, 1897

It is more difficult than I thought. Getting ready for a floating expedition necessitates packing lightly because there is not a lot of room on a raft. For some reason this vaguely gives me the impression that I can just throw a few pair of underwear and shirts in a bag and be good to go. Alas, when you are forced to pack light, it becomes harder, not easier. Economizing space is a specific skill, and when it comes right down to it I find myself overwhelmed at gathering together everything we need.

Also, I am under some time constraints. I've just returned from a speaking engagement in Washington, D.C., and the great Smith River journey is following quickly on its heels. All the time I spent prepping my engagement in our nation's capital is time I was not spending getting ready. Friday before our departure is fairly miserable, as it involves a lot of shopping. I hate shopping when it isn't the leisurely kind of shopping. It wears me out having to go to five different stores to obtain five things I need right now, rather than accumulating it over a longer period of time. My preference usually is to just click a button on *Amazon.com* and have it on my doorstep in two days. But one pays for procrastination by way of desperately rushing to multiple local stores looking for that one single thing you need.

Saturday morning arrives, and it is hectic. I have some sudden banking to do, in anticipation of a credit card bill coming due while I'm away, and so Ty takes it upon himself to load up our truck. We've already gathered everything we need on my garage floor, so while I am otherwise detained he makes sure everything is packed. Suddenly, he remembers he needs something else, so he takes off in my vehicle to the store.

Around 10:30 we finally pull out of my drive and make

it about three blocks when I say, "Hey Ty, did you remember your pistol?" He has, in fact, left it in my vehicle after his little side trip. Off to a flying stop, we turn around to retrieve it. This is necessary for a couple of reasons: first, we can't just leave his Springfield XD .45 caliber in my parked vehicle for thieves to find. Second, my 9 millimeter Beretta does not exactly have the same heft when it comes to, say, shooting at a bear. A 9mm will just irritate a Grizzly, but a .45 might just stop it cold, if it came to that.

Bears are not the only consideration, of course. In Big Sky Country one does not carry firearms for just *foreseeable* uses, but rather the uses you cannot anticipate (which is why we roll our eyes at urban elite types who are always telling us what kind of guns we *don't* "need"). Texas Ranger Woodrow F. Call in *Lonesome Dove* puts it best: "Better to have it and not need it than to need it and not have it." It is true that in the case of a Grizzly bear a pistol is a "last resort" sort of thing; but, hey, Meryl Streep's character in *The River Wild* didn't expect to get kidnapped by bank robbers on *her* rafting trip adventure. So there's that.

---

So getting out of Billings seems like an arduous task in and of itself. We finally drive up Zimmerman Trail, a still navigable (and now paved) 19th-century Stagecoach route that winds up through the long line of imposing sandstone bluffs on the north side of town. These bluffs are technically called "buttes," but locals call them the "Rimrocks" (or "Rims" for short) because they form a huge rim bordering the north side of the Yellowstone River valley. High up on the Rimrocks is where the airport is, and one can survey the entire, breathtaking valley: 60 miles directly south are the dark, volcanic-looking Pryor Mountains with its herds of wild Mustang horses sired from Spanish and Portuguese stallions over 200 years ago; 60 miles to the southwest is the mighty Beartooth range, with its prototypical Rocky Mountain snowcapped peaks; to the east, the river winds its way past Pompey's Pillar, a rock outcropping that features the only physical evidence of Lewis and Clark's famous journey (William Clark chiseled his autograph into it); and endlessly to the north is prairie as far as the eye can see.

Allow me a few words in defense of this particular spot on the Montana map. Billings, Montana is a geographical accident. They call it the "Magic City" because it seemed to spring up *sua sponte.* What happened was that in 1882 the tycoons of the *Northern Pacific Railway,* sitting in their Lordly offices in Minneapolis and surveying a map of their dominions, simply decreed that at the eastern end of the Yellowstone River valley, "Let there be a railroad junction and city!" And, by *fiat*, it was so. They named the city after their former president (who had been dismissed by the board a year earlier), Frederick H. Billings, a Vermonter who led a fascinating life that involved making his way to San Francisco during the Gold Rush of '49. There he had inadvertently named another city when, upon cresting the hill and seeing the bay, he quoted a poetic verse from English philosopher George Berkeley. So Berkeley, California was named. Today the City of Billings is the largest in Montana, population 110,000, and a major center of industry: railroads, of course, (although most of that has been moved 15 miles west to the outlying city of Laurel), agriculture, law, and medicine.

And it is sneered at by snobs inhabiting the rest of the state. Billings lacks the sex appeal of, say, Bozeman or Missoula. Of course it is cooler to have your settlement invented by a trailblazing mountain man rather than a rich railroad tycoon. Bozeman and Missoula are both nestled right in the mountains and have very scenic sight lines. For both of those cities, ski mountains are minutes away, as are blue ribbon trout streams. Both are major university towns, and boast all the trendy things that come with college towns—bohemian dive bars, stores offering "organic" everything-you-can-imagine, vinyl record shops, and the like. If you want to be a pothead, Wiccan, ski bum, and/or progressive socialist, those are better destinations. Except that, ahem: Billings has more craft breweries and distilleries. Take that, Western Montana hipsters.

I'm biased, of course, but here's my view: Billings

really is “Montana’s Trailhead.” If you’re in Bozeman or Missoula or Kalispell, you’re going to get your mountain experience. But Billings is unique because it sits right on a spectacular geological seam: immediately to the southwest, all the mountain experiences you could imagine—day hikes and 12-thousand-foot peaks—in the one-million-square-mile playground we call the Absaroka-Beartooth Wilderness; immediately to the north and east, the glorious, sweeping Great Plains underneath the biggest cathedral sky you’ve ever seen. Billings is the better spot on the map because, as Anne Shirley of *Green Gables* would say, it gives more “scope to the imagination.”

---

TRUTH BE TOLD, I almost never go north. As we cruise the highway under brilliant sunlight through sweeping “amber waves of grain,” I am once again enamored with Big Sky Country. We are leaving our cultured, urban confines (yes, Billings is quite cultured) and reentering the world of big pickup trucks (we ourselves occupy an F-150), cowboy hats, and barbed wire. We even rekindle my youth by playing classic Garth Brooks tracks on the radio. This is endless ranch land dotted by numerous small settlements without traffic lights: Acton, Broadview, Lavina, Ryegate, and Harlowton. I don’t get out this way often enough. Coming from my world of studying western civilization and its upheavals, the simple quiet of these communities makes it seem a different world altogether.

In some places it really is a different world, as we pass by a number of Hutterite colonies—the remaining descendants of 16th century German Anabaptist Reformer Jacob Hutter. The Hutterites are now a small, insular (and, as is fairly well known, somewhat inbred) community that shelters itself from the outer world, but they are not so doctrinaire as their Amish brethren in Pennsylvania. They continue to speak a sort of pigeon German, but they embrace modern technology like trucks and agricultural equipment. Their agricultural operations are impressive, and they provide local communities, even a metropolis like Billings, with a great deal of produce. This is the first time on our journey that the question of my relationship to the wider world strikes me. The Hutterites have their way, in a typically extreme Anabaptist fashion. But it seems utterly pragmatic at its core: reject the world as evil, but use its technology anyway? Make no mistake: the Amish are every bit as pragmatic (buggies and plows are a man-made technology, after all), but using outdated things at least gives a better appearance of having the courage of their convictions.

Internally, Hutterites form communist societies, which just means their free markets are of the "black" variety. Once upon a time my father got permission to hunt deer on Hutterite land. Their leader, Jake (Nearly all

Hutterite males are named after their long-distant ancestor), asked only one thing in compensation: a bottle of *Canadian Club* whiskey, which he then—eyes narrowly shifting from side to side—implored my Dad to keep just between themselves. As in all communist societies, some people are more "equal" than others.

All this "Man vs. The World" got me thinking as we made our way to our first destination, which I discovered was another long-lost civilization: Neihart, Montana. And my thoughts then flowered into the related question of "Man vs. Nature."

---

NEIHART IS BARELY a spot on the map. Nestled in a steep valley along the main thoroughfare through the Little Belt Mountains, you will miss it if you blink for a moment or two. There is no cell phone service in Neihart. It once boasted a population of 10,000 in the heyday of its mining industry; today, the population is exactly 32. And Ty has known two pillars of this community nearly all his life: Royal and Nancy Westervelt. Retired ranchers from the remote Montana "highline," they now own and operate the *Neihart Inconvenience Store*. This quaint establishment is exactly what you might imagine: a general store carrying just about anything you might need, from canned goods to bottles of wine and DVDs for cold winter nights when you have nothing better to do. In our case, we dig out a frozen pizza and bake it for lunch.

Immediately to the left as you walk in the door is a large dinette table, which seems to be the community center. At any given time of day you'll find locals sitting here reading the *Great Falls Tribune* and engaging in small talk. These are weathered people with deep lines of hard experience etched on their faces. Somehow the years of hard labor in unforgiving elements has not eroded their senses of humor, even if it is at times a rather dark and cynical sense. They smile and laugh a great deal. Sitting well above a mile over sea level, Neihart experiences punishing winters with subzero temperatures and mountains of snow. Which makes its mining heritage all the more incredible.

The valley remains littered with ancient mining works: ground up tailings, rusted implements, and shuttered shafts. Just outside of Royal and Nancy's house across the road from the store is a large hole dug straight into the rock. Olivia and I climb in to take a look. Somebody at some point had started a mine shaft, only to abandon it thirty or forty feet in. We collect some souvenir rocks, and it occurs to me: whoever did this did it *with a pick axe.*

It is so alien a thought it seems like those of generations ago were a different species altogether. Is there anything into which our decadent, convenience-worshipping society would put that much work? I cannot think of it. Our technology is an unqualified blessing—more productivity with a fraction of the labor—but something is lost. There are always tradeoffs. How much more could human civilization achieve if, alongside our ever-growing efficiency, we kept the same intensity of labor that caused a man to pick axe his way forty feet into solid rock? Alas, perhaps human nature hasn't changed as much as I think. After all, this shaft was abandoned. Whether through laziness, despair, or lack of fruitfulness, I will never know.

We retrieve two four-wheel all-terrain vehicles: Ty on one, Olivia behind me on the other. We are in for a thrill. Cold wind in our faces, we blast up old, abandoned mining roads, dodging branches and bear scat, bouncing over fallen trees, careening around switchback S-curves, higher and higher, all the way to the top of one of the many Little Belt Mountains where the air is cold enough for June snow. Looking into valleys, we see the remnants of this lost civilization everywhere: mining remains (tailings) and equipment just abandoned where pine forests now encroach to conceal them.

What kinds of people were these? "Go West, Young Man," types, I suppose, off to make their fortunes in the rugged wilds. These must have been brutal and very short lives. All sorts of motives undoubtedly mixed—greed, independence, carelessness with the environment, perhaps out of malice or sheer need for survival—and yet I cannot help but see some nobility. I am witnessing remnants of some kind of cultivation, marks of human hands on God's works. This was the original mandate, after all: to cultivate, rule, and subdue creation. This effort can be twisted in so many ways, yet the glory of humanity's original charter cannot be totally effaced. I see trash in the form of rusted metal, yes; but I also see creativity and ingenuity and effort that speaks to the uniqueness of human beings made as the image of their Maker. This all begs a question: what is and what ought to be our relationship to nature?

I spend five days in the wilderness, yet none of it truly "untouched" because *I am there*. If you really think about it, none of the places we want to preserve for our recreation and enjoyment, national forests, parks, or nature preserves, are really untouched or pristine. We know about them, care for them, and, yes, cultivate them precisely because we humans touch these places. The ancient Zen koan, "If a tree falls in the forest and nobody is around to hear it, does it make a sound?" is not really a silly question. Paradoxically, it raises deep questions about our relationship to the natural world. Is it meant to exist independently of us? Does nature have intrinsic meaning apart from our interaction? Does nature somehow need human persons, or is the ideal "state of nature" one in which humans dare not tread?

This is not the first time in our journey these questions occur to me, and more and more I see that collectively we are of two minds. We talk about pure nature as though its ideal is little-to-no human involvement (on the extreme, we have the "human beings are a cancer on the Earth" crowd), but then we act a bit differently. Time and again on our river journey we are told to camp "without a trace," or "as if you were never there." And yet, the same United States Forest Service proselytizing this ideal has set up boat camps all down the river for humans to occupy and enjoy. These are outfitted with fire pits, trails, and—yes, really—latrines. Not particularly nice ones: essentially a toilet sitting on a hole in the ground in the open air. Human cultivation at its most primitive.

Herein lies a paradox. There is something deep within us that cannot "let nature be." If a tree falls in the forest, we want to know about it and the reasons why (clear cutting or bark beetles?) and what we can or should do about it. We yearn to be a part of nature, to experience it, to interpret it, to be awed by it. And we instinctively know—the latrines testify!—this "being part of" carries with it responsibilities. It was the dog in Jack London's story who felt the *The Call of the Wild*, but we feel a call to tame the wild. It is, in fact, a vocation. It is primeval. We tell good tales of leaving pristine nature to itself, but the impulses to cultivate and shape, to interpret, to name, to leave a mark testifies to our creation as *imago Dei*. Sub-creators, cultivators, interpreters, speakers.

Interestingly enough, Jacob Hutter's 16th century contemporary John Calvin wrote that God has left vestiges of himself in all of his created world and that there is nothing that lacks at least some spark of his divinity. This conviction led to the opposite of Hutter's isolated and closed communities; it led instead to a vibrant engagement of the world—not just in the natural sciences, but politics, art, law, engineering, and commerce. Taking root in Holland and England—and moving from there to the North American continent—Calvinism was a catalyst for an explosion of innovation and prosperity the likes of which had never been seen in human history. In many ways Calvin's view of the natural order (it isn't *evil*) made the very modern world the Hutterites are forced to uncomfortably co-opt for their survival. We bear God's likeness, and so we, too, love to make—and leave—our mark.

We practice our own unique signatures. We build monuments to testify to our posterity of our existence. We bury time capsules and hurl records of our great works of art into the furthest reaches of space. We get tattoos, personalized plates, and nicknames; we ©, ®, and ™; we ink-stain our unique fingerprints; we stamp, seal, and emboss; we brand the flesh of livestock and turn our very identities into personal "brands" of a different kind; we abandon our mine shafts for others to find; carve initials into trees, rocks like Pompey's Pillar, and bathroom stalls; we dig fire pits, clear trails, and put toilets in the open air in the middle of forests.

So much for "without a trace." We are humans. We are irrepressibly hardwired to make our mark. We are a part of nature, and in a profound way apart *from* nature. We sometimes feel like strangers looking in, yet looking in at something familiar. We have the breath of life, inhabitants of the spiritual world. But we are also formed of dust: hence, our affinity for the elements. From the "outside," as it were, we act on the raw materials of the world not with sheer instinct, but with something much more transcendent: intention, meaning, and purpose. Robert Noyce didn't just see a dark gray crystalline substance called silicon; he envisioned silicon transistors strung together conducting electricity on a flat silicon sheet: the first integrated circuit that became Intel's microchip.

Someone once said that God made man erect that he might look heavenward, while four-footed beasts only look down. That seems true, as far as it goes, but we look down just as much as the four-footed beasts. But differently. Nature is not just "there" for us, something we take for granted. We see, as if from some transcendent vantage point, not just stuff, but untapped potential; not just what our environment is, but what it might become under our mastery. We are *imago Dei*—the image of God. I think wrapped up in the *Shorter Catechism's* "chief end" is this: responsibly making *our* mark for God's glory is not to contaminate nature; it is to adorn it.

It is what we are for.

## 2

## FATHERHOOD & FUNYUNS

"Jean Valjean knew no more than she where they were going, trusting to God as she trusted to himself."

— VICTOR HUGO, LES MISÉRABLES

Inspiring, isn't it? If only we weren't all such bumbling incompetents. Enter Stage Left: The Fall, Original Sin, Crooked Sticks, and all that. As we approach the highway junction to head "up the hill" to Neihart, I casually ask:

"Say, Ty, did you throw in those two life jackets for Livie and me?"

Pause.

"Um, I don't think so. Where were those?"

"Right there in the garage with all the rest of the stuff."

"Huh."

Pause.

"Say, Ty, did you remember to throw in the camp stove?"

"Um, I don't remember seeing that. Where was it?"

"Right there in the garage with all the rest of the stuff."

Pause.

Ty: "Come to think of it, what did I do with my rain gear?"

On and on this goes for a few miles, as the realization dawns that we have essentially left half our equipment in my garage. And, of course, we had already returned to my garage when Ty had to get his pistol. Feeling like complete idiots, we pull over while we've still got cell service to tell Nancy we would have to return the two hours back to Billings. She assures us that the (superbly named) *Neihart Inconvenience Store* would be able to outfit us. At her urging, we press on.

Thus is the motto for our motley expedition born: "We suck at this." A truer motto was never spoken. None of us have ever done anything like a multi-day river float on a sluggish raft loaded down with gear through a mountain canyon. And we are not off to a very good start.

To add insult to this extreme injury to our pride, later in the afternoon we take our leave of Neihart to make our way to the campground from which we would launch the following morning. Nancy clearly instructs us to go up to the house to retrieve the life jackets. So, naturally, we jump in the truck and head straight for the campground. We *really* suck at this.

Late afternoon we've arrived at Camp Baker, the U.S. Forest Service campground from which all Smith River floaters must embark. Our tent set up, I muse aloud: "I don't think we remembered the life jackets. Again." No problem. Nancy will be sure to bring them in the morning. Right? Along with packing all the life jackets and food and sleeping bags and tents and pots and pans and utensils and toilet paper and bug spray and coolers and ice for the other ten people she's bringing. Right? Yeah, she'll remember.

Back in the truck, we are heading toward White Sulphur Springs. I've got two cell phones open in the my lap, trying to get some service. Ty's got AT&T; I've got Verizon. Perfect test for all those boastful "most coverage" claims. AT&T wins! Ty gets a single bar and calls Nancy. She assures us she'll bail us out again by remembering, as we cannot seem to, our life jackets. We press on to White Sulphur Springs anyway, because we are hungry and have no camp stove on which to cook. Also the dry ice we put in our Yeti cooler has literally frozen all of our other food solid. Did I mention we really suck at this?

Soggy convenience store burgers are really nasty, but if you eat one in the right context, like now, it tastes delicious. Livie and I browse around for some chips or something to go with them.

"Dad, let's get some Funyuns!"

"*Funyuns*!? *FUNYUNS!?* How about a little PROTEIN, Jesse?"

She laughs.

Here there is some backstory that takes us into yet another dimension of our tale: Fatherhood.

---

HAVING children has fallen on hard times. Collectively, we seem to have adopted George Bailey's bad attitude in *It's a Wonderful Life*: "You call this a happy family? Why do we have to have all these kids?" In his brilliant book, *What To Expect When No One's Expecting*, Jonathan Last reveals the simultaneously hilarious, yet disquieting fact that in the affluent suburb of Washington, D.C. where he lives there are numerous clothing stores. For dogs. In this same suburb one looks in vain to find a store that sells clothes for actual human children. No doubt there are lots of deep reasons the birthrate in America and the Western world at large is dismal—the narcissism of the sexual revolution comes to mind—but one practical explanation does loom large: kids are a pain.

Children are a gigantic responsibility. They are completely helpless. You have to teach them absolutely everything—except how to say, "No!" They cry for no reason whatsoever. They whine incessantly. They are constantly hungry. They soil their diapers. Yes, there are the occasional sweet moments. It's best to keep your iPhone readily accessible to capture those for your Instagram feed. After all, we want the world to think our kids are 99% bundles of joy when, in fact, the percentage is not nearly so high.

I know well the selfish impulse to put off introducing little barbarians into your comfortable life. My bride and I were three years into our happy marriage, and our life together was terrific. We were doing just fine. We were best friends. We were fulfilled. We didn't exactly feel an overwhelming desire to add a third wheel to our well-oiled lives. The classic, passionate tale went something like this:

"You know, Brian, if we do this right now I'm going to get pregnant."

"Oh, no you won't. Trust me, baby!"

Baby, indeed. Nine months later, Olivia arrived.

It was not like I expected. You might think, as I vaguely did in my weaker moments, that adding a third person into a happy marriage would introduce competition. You can't help but think that love, time, attention, happiness, and joy are scarce resources. And if you spread scarce resources too widely you will inevitably experience their dilution. After all, now all the wonderful time you had for each other is taken up in nursing, changing diapers, sitting up in the middle of the night trying to rock the dry, well-fed, yet nevertheless screaming brat back to sleep, and so on. Domestic tranquility will never be tranquil again. There just has to be a loss, doesn't there?

I slowly discovered something, and I've felt it more deeply with the successive arrivals of my other two girls: love does not dilute. Adding a third, and a fourth, and a fifth to our family resulted in exponential increase. What was added to our home was not at all primarily "burden" or "another mouth to feed." Rather, a *person* was added. It is as though your two-dimensional world becomes three dimensional. You were happy enough with a black and white world, and along comes Technicolor. You thought life was exciting, but suddenly the added texture makes your former existence look flat and uninteresting by comparison.

"God is love," wrote the Apostle John. Think of that. God—Father, Son, and Holy Spirit—is an infinite and eternal fountain of self-giving and receiving. He never diminishes, never dilutes. Love is life-giving. There is a creaturely analogy here, and it makes sense that when we as a society stopped really believing in God we started believing the lie that love is a scarce resource subject to the natural course of entropy. Reality is (because God is real!) that what I thought might diminish my happiness —having to give more of myself these little intruders— exponentially increased my happiness.

And that happiness has increasing stages all its own. With Olivia, it started small, just like her size. We lived in a row house in inner-city Philadelphia. I remember kicking back on the La-Z-Boy watching the Phillies on our tiny television set, my tiny newborn fast asleep on my chest. That shallow, rapid breathing, our hearts beating together. This was a regular scene, evidenced by the fact that "baseball" was her fourth word, right behind "Dada," "Mama," and "Kitty."

Happiness, along with all its subsidiary branches like joy, satisfaction, pride, surprise, and amazement, grew right along with her. Walking for miles and miles along the streets of Aberdeen, Scotland playing a re-tooled game of "Slug Bug." In America, the game involves spotting Volkswagen Beetles and yelling "Slug Bug!" In Scotland we changed it to Mini Cooper, since that was by far the more ubiquitous automobile. She would run ahead along Union Street, peeking her head around corners of side streets, yelling "Mini!" with delight and wild abandon. We never let her win. She destroyed us at this game all on her own. She could spot the familiar curve of a Mini Cooper fender parked in the middle of a huge row of cars a quarter mile away.

She eventually became a reader, artist, pianist, the youngest Ham radio operator in the state of Montana, and much more. She is a person that grew to be a subject of such interest to me. Her endless dissection of the Harry Potter novels, poems that she wrote, her dabbling in calligraphy—all of this is such an incredible enrichment of the world that my original native worries that adding her to our lives would be a subtraction seems insane. It *is* insane. An insanity that has all but gripped our modern world, if the ready availability of doggy clothing stores is any indication. All of the burden or effort expended to raise this marvelous creature redounded to *our* benefit for this reason: love does not dilute. It creates an overflowing surplus.

The same is true of my other children, but in such a variety of enriching ways that I dare not bore you by recounting them. And who knows? In time they may get their own story.

---

Back to Funyuns.

Now is one of those uncomfortable times in our story that I must feel the heat from judgmental eyes, and lose the respect of lots of religious folks on the conservative end of the spectrum—my people, essentially. I have found that there is a lot about parenting that isn't strictly in the user's manual. Oh, certainly the Bible tells us enough about ethics and morals and how to parent children, but it's more a framework within which we get to exercise wisdom than it is a compendium of casuistry.

Enough throat clearing.

Livie and I are watching AMC's hit series, *Breaking Bad*. I'll grant that it's a pretty raw and "adult" kind of show for a fourteen-year-old, and there are a few (surprisingly few, actually) scenes that get self-edited with the fast-forward button. It is also my favorite motion picture series of all time. For the uninitiated, *Breaking Bad* tells the saga—the Greek tragedy, really—of high school science teacher Walter White. After Walter is diagnosed with lung cancer, he teams up with his former student, drug dealer Jesse Pinkman, ostensibly out of panic that he isn't leaving his family enough money. Using his extraordinary education in chemistry, Walter concocts the purest strain of methamphetamine anyone has ever seen.

The story is of the classic "rise and fall" variety, and is full of incredible characters played by incredible actors. Walter and Jesse eventually build a drug empire, always just out of the reach of Walter's dogged brother-in-law, DEA Special Agent Hank Schrader. As you might imagine, this show depicts a great deal of the dark underbelly of the drug trafficking trade.

When Walter and Jesse arrive at their first serious "cook" session in Middle-of-Nowhere, New Mexico, in their beat up RV, it was Jesse's job to bring the necessary food. And, I'll be honest: I'm now resonating with bumbling incompetence. Jesse brought—you guessed it —little individual bags of Funyuns.

*"Funyuns? FUNYUNS!? How about a little PROTEIN, Jesse?"*

---

We've never actually tried Funyuns, but I am all for it. I quickly ascertain that they are made to resemble onion rings, but the only onion involved is powder applied in seemingly (well, literally) industrial amounts. It is actually just a cornmeal crisp shaped like a fried onion ring. The texture is basically like a pork rind—salty styrofoam. After knocking down a quarter of the bag we are very sympathetic to Walter White. We just don't see the attraction.

I digress. What could possibly make me believe my 14-year-old daughter should watch *Breaking Bad* with me? It's fairly simple, I suppose. My daughters are home-schooled. They are bright, accomplished, and well-adjusted. Unlike lots of kids in public school environments, they are fairly comfortable talking to people of all ages rather than just their peers. But they are not exactly what you'd call streetwise.

Olivia is signed up to attend high school this fall for her freshman year, her first time in a school environment. She has really good core group of girls from our church she'll be attending with, so I'm not worried about falling in with the wrong crowd. And she's not particularly interested in boys yet, either, but I'm keeping my eyes peeled for signs of that. She and I have a little inside joke we got from a Facebook advertisement, a T-Shirt that prints a little "Dad's Guide To Daughters Dating." It goes like this: "Shoot the first one. Word will spread." Olivia is so cool she wanted to buy one, not for me, but for her to wear. Alas, they didn't have any women's sizes.

There are some things I want Olivia to see and hear before heading off to a large high school. I want her to get a "feel" for how people talk and how they act. She's a pretty devoted Christian kid and has spent her life in a closely knit Christian community. I don't want her first reaction to sustained exposure to the dress, the slang, the jokes, the profanity of others to be debilitating to her. I want her to be comfortable in her own skin as she moves through the world, and it's hard to be comfortable if you're shocked and outraged all the time.

Enter Jesse Pinkman, the extremely good looking, witty, profane, wannabe gangster with baggy pants, oversized coat, and ballcap all akimbo. And his drug abuse with the misery and squalor involved in worshiping and serving that particular idol. Enter his tweaker friends and, despite their humor and other human qualities, their basic shallowness. Enter the crude jokes, the innuendo, the things young men think and talk about 24/7/365. And, Enter: discovering the ability to occasionally find redeeming qualities in even the most wretched of the earth. And Enter: watching how Walter White's tiny, prideful lies blossom to the point of no return and his ultimate downfall.

Fictional stories are incredible tools. We inhabit and experience worlds vicariously and learn from them. *Breaking Bad* allows my daughter to experience the dark sides of the world right alongside her Dad in the safe harbor of our own home. We get to debrief about the characters, their motives and actions, their sins and failures. She gets to learn how the world works in a controlled environment before being thrown into the uncontrolled one.

Someone once gave me a profound illustration of what it's like trying to prepare kids for life in a world filled with depravity. It's the spiritual equivalent of preparing kids for life in a world filled with biological disease: we vaccinate them. The process of vaccination is pretty simple: give a child a controlled dose of an inoperable foreign virus and their bodies miraculously learn to resist the real ones in the future. We build an immunity to hostile outside influences that aim to destroy us. So, too, with our souls; controlled exposure to hostile outside influences builds an immunity to those influences. That's the theory, and I think it is elegant and makes perfect sense.

There's more to it, of course. Just as the body needs healthy cells to expel invaders, one must positively fill one's soul with truth, goodness, and beauty. Early American theologian Jonathan Edwards called it the "expulsive power of a new affection." You have to cultivate good affections in order to inoculate against bad ones. But controlled exposure is still part of the equation.

What happens when a young teenager encounters depravity and it is wholly *de novo*, radically new and heretofore never even conceived in their hearts or minds? Perhaps shock and revulsion, at first. But novelty is a powerful attractant that embeds itself in the mind and is able to slowly overcome even the most violent initial reaction. I want my girls to be *wise*—to know such things and to know the truth about them. To know the attractions of sin, and, more importantly, their deceptions.

This is partly why I never lie to my kids about things like smoking. It is a lie to tell children that smoking is "terrible." Oh, yes, objectively it is a stinky, nasty, expensive, and unhealthy habit. It is "terrible" in that sense. But hundreds of millions, if not billions, of people around the globe do not smoke because it is terrible; they smoke because it is *wonderful*. I do not tell my daughter that she will hate it if she ever tries a cigarette; one deep inhale and, after a brief fit of coughing, my lie will be readily apparent. Not only will my credibility be shattered, but a whole new nefarious world will open up for her. So I tell her that she will *love* it; and there—right there—is the trap that can and usually does lead to a (shorter) lifetime of burdensome addiction, one of the most difficult to overcome.

We actually have a conversation about smoking. She says, "Don't worry, Dad: I'll *never* smoke." And, another time, "Don't worry, Dad: I'll *never* get drunk." I wave her rash promises away:

"Sweetheart, I appreciate your assurances. But you are making the promises of a 14-year old. I know temptations you have never felt. You have not yet met that cute boy you desperately want to impress at the party."

Thoughtful pause.

"That's true, Dad."

"Livie, I'm trying to prepare you for the temptations you don't even know about yet. So don't make 14-year-old promises your 18-year-old self might struggle to keep. Let's take things day by day and rely on God's grace to be wise at all times."

I feel like I'm on solid ground here. I'm using my own considerable experience with temptation to counsel the neophyte to beware. The Bible says that Jesus himself was tempted like us in every way, yet without sin. And because of his temptations and suffering, he is able to sympathize with our weakness. Sympathize. That's amazing, if you think about it. Lots of people instinctively think that Jesus had it far easier than us. After all, he is the God-Man and surely he had a power to resist that we lack.

But C.S. Lewis brilliantly points out that Jesus actually had it far worse because he alone knows the real depth and power of temptation. You see, we fallen, sinful, crooked people cave in at the Devil's slightest suggestion, only to later moan and wail that the temptation was *irresistible*. We have no idea what we are talking about. How would we know what "irresistible" is if the Devil never has to turn the pressure knob past Level 1? I once preached a sermon on this, and my second daughter drew a picture for her notes. It was a mechanical device called a "Tempt-O-Matic." On it was a lever with two helpful labels: "Maximum" or "Pathetic." We cave at pathetic, but Jesus felt the maximum. He resisted, and yet —incredibly—he doesn't laugh at us; he sympathizes with us.

What grace.

We *are* bumbling incompetents, about much more than just forgetting camping gear. Fallen into original sin, crooked sticks, and all that. But on this night, huddled into our tent at Camp Baker in sub-freezing temperatures, I am warm with love and affection for my daughter, and hopeful, too. We have amazing resources of special grace to help us in this journey of life.

And everyday, ordinary graces like fatherhood and daughterhood, *Breaking Bad,* convenience store hamburgers, and, yes, Funyuns. But not as your sole source of protein.

3

## PEACE LIKE A RIVER

> "Drinking beer with friends is perhaps the most underestimated of all Reformation insights and essential to ongoing reform; wasting time with a choice friend or two on a regular basis might be the best investment you ever make."
>
> — Carl Trueman

A quarter-inch layer of frost covers the cooler after a frigid night at Camp Baker. Obeying that universal impulse to make our mark on nature, Ty scrawls a commemorative message in the frost with his finger and photographs it: "Smith River, 6-11-2017." It was frigid, indeed. Our tent is not really the cold weather variety. There is a mesh window that, unlike other tents, does not zip closed but instead is simply covered by the rain fly. Moisture is clinging to the fabric on the inside of the tent—condensation from the deep breathing of three people practically freezing to death. We worry a bit about what this forebodes for the rest of our trip, as there are adverse weather conditions in the forecast.

But the weather the morning of launch day is glorious. Our muscles and bones ache from sleeping on the ground, but the brightly shining sun helps to get us warm. As does a cup of instant coffee. Instant coffee is always terrible, but we find that the tiny Starbucks packets are far less terrible than other brands. We use a tiny backpacking stove that we actually have remembered to bring to heat the water. Olivia begins her practice of making her signature "Campstove Mocha": the budding barista just blends a packet of hot chocolate with the packet of coffee. Surprisingly good.

Now things begin to get hectic. We have already the night before pumped up our raft and put together the rack with three seats that attach to the top, and now is time to figure out how we are to load everything. In our haste to leave Billings, we really just tried to make sure all our gear was in the truck along with us. Hilarious disconnect between intention and execution, I know. But now we must actually pack all of our belongings into "dry bags," ingenious waterproof storage containers. By the end, we have no room to spare in the dry bags, and no room to spare on the raft itself.

Ty's cooler does not fit in the raft. Of course. It's a

Mammoth Brand, and I guess they mean it. Royal and Nancy are bringing a smaller cooler we can use as a companion to our Yeti, which we are borrowing from our friend Joe along with his raft. A quick word about Yeti coolers. I have long scoffed at the unbelievable expense of what I perceive to be simple insulated plastic containers. How one could spend $700 to $1,000 on a cooler has until now been beyond my comprehension. I've already mentioned how our dry ice froze everything solid in the cooler. Five days later everything in the cooler is as cold as it would be in your refrigerator at home. I have no idea what Yeti has done to achieve these results, but it's sheer wizardry.

These types of premium coolers are not optional, either. It is a matter of keeping our food cold for days on end, sure; but they provide the more important service of keeping bears away from our food.

---

MUCH LIKE FOREIGNERS visiting Yellowstone National Park, people visiting Montana from large urban centers find it difficult to take warning signs seriously. Every campground in every National Forest and Wilderness Area features signs that read: "Danger: Grizzly Country," along with specific instructions on what not to do, and for some strange psychological reason people refuse to believe it. I suppose that since the vast majority of people have never seen a Grizzly bear, the subconscious mind finds it too otherworldly, too unreal to comprehend.

I myself have only seen one Grizzly bear in the wild at a distance, and I was in the safety of a vehicle. I am certain, though, that I have had some very close calls. I imagine that in heaven I will discover just how often God protected me in my folly. For example, when I was eighteen my friend Noah and I took a 30-mile backpacking trip out of Cooke City into Slough Creek to scout it for elk hunting. Slough Creek is a major drainage to the north of Yellowstone National Park, and every year hundreds, if not thousands, of elk migrate northward. Our trail was 15-miles each way, straight into completely unpopulated and uncivilized country.

I believe we both carried pistols, but incredibly we did not have bear spray (which is the safer and often effective option). We parked our car at the trailhead next to a grove of deep brush. Noah was digging around in the front seat of the car for something, and I was pulling packs out of our little hatchback. Suddenly, the bushes rustled and a magnificent bull moose twice the height of our little car—with antlers *wider* than our little car—came tearing out of the brush. He stopped right in front of the engine, glared straight at me, eyes red with anger; he snorted, stomped his foot, and then hightailed it away into the woods. It happened so fast that Noah barely saw his backside as he disappeared.

Did this make me reconsider the adventure? Not in

the slightest, even though it is well known that moose are often more dangerous than bears. They don't tear your flesh with claws and teeth: they just stomp you to death in an insane rage. Foolishly undeterred, we packed up and walked into the wilderness fifteen miles.

At points the danger began to dawn on me. I remember creeping on a narrow path in the hot afternoon, weaving through bushes full of berries. There was bear scat everywhere, so fresh it was practically steaming. I hope I only imagined that it was. By this point we felt there was no turning back, and by God's grace we pressed on and did make it to Slough Creek without incident.

We found an outfitters camp that had a ready-made fire pit. We were so exhausted, and the weather was so fair that we decided to forego setting up our tent. After we ate dinner, we simply laid out our sleeping bags next to a warm fire and stared up, dumbfounded, at a sky unlike anything we'd ever seen. There was no artificial light for at least 15 miles as the crow flies in any direction. There was no moon. The entire Milky Way galaxy was spread out overhead, a scene not easily forgotten.

We were disappointed that we hadn't seen any elk or any real sign of elk. The fire was dying down and Noah grabbed a stick and started stirring the coals. The sparks shot up into the sky and in that instant we froze. In a 360-degree circle around us, elk started a deafening chorus of bugling. They were many, and they were close. We were mesmerized, but honestly we were also a little frightened.

We felt like intruders in this primitive wilderness, and in all likelihood things more threatening than elk were out there in the darkness: bears, or even a wolf pack fresh up from the Park.

So it is not just tourists and city-slickers who can be foolish when it comes to wildlife. But sometimes it has nothing to do with folly. Yes, seemingly every single year we Montanans will roll our eyes at the inevitable idiot who gets himself gored by a Bison while visiting the Park (the caretakers cannot possibly put up *more* signs telling people: Do NOT approach Bison!), but other times there is nobody at fault. A few years back a Grizzly sow and her cubs attacked visitors in their tents in a busy, well-cultivated campground outside of Cooke City. One man was killed and two others were severely injured. It meant death for the bears, too, once officers from Fish & Wildlife finally tracked them down—the cubs, too. Sadly, once they have the taste for humans, their behavior cannot be corrected.

This is thankfully a rare occurrence, but this is very serious business. When the Forest Service says they want coolers "bear-proof" (as in, they do not emit odors), they are not joking.

---

Our entire party of fourteen is supposed to meet with the Park Ranger at 9:00. It's 8:45 and still no Westervelts or anybody else from Neihart. The caravan finally arrives in the nick of time, and we all pile in to the Ranger station to sign our names, pay our launch fee, and get the customary lecture about something called "micro-trash" and camping "without a trace." We receive permit tags to attach to the sterns of our vessels and are cleared to launch.

Now trucks and trailers are moving all over, getting rafts to the water. People are running every which way. We are double checking, triple checking, quadruple checking that we have every single thing we are going to need for the next few days. If you forget it, you will simply not have it. I'm wearing my prescription sunglasses and I have to rack my brain: Did I put my regular glasses in my bag that is buried deep inside a dry bag? Or did I inadvertently leave them in the cab of the pickup truck? I cannot say for certain. Our raft is sitting on the launch, and others are waiting for their turn. They'll just have to wait. I jog all the way to the parking lot where the truck is because at this point a simple process of elimination is easier than digging things out of dry bags. No glasses in the truck, which I choose to believe means they are in the depths of a dry bag.

And so, blood pressure at high levels, a bit of fear and trepidation, Olivia takes her seat high in the stern, Ty takes his seat at the oars situated midship, and I push us off into the water and clamber over the side into my post at the bow. The raft sags in the water, gear groans, and the water swiftly begins pushing us along. Ty pulls us to the other bank to wait a few minutes to make sure our whole party gets launched, but there isn't any need as Royal, Nancy, and their grandchildren go cruising right past us. I guess it's time to go!

The first turn is 150 yards away and veers to starboard. We can still hear the racket from the campground: trucks roaring, people yelling to each other, clinking, clacking, banging, and the like. We gently curve around the bend, and...

Total peace.

A funny thing about floating on a river that hadn't occurred to me before. When you are next to a river, as I usually am with my fly rod, you *hear* the river, the gentle steady roar of waters rushing by. When you are carried along with those waters, you do not hear the roar; you are part of it. On a raft you hear the gentle splish-splash of water caressing the side of the boat, or the splash of oars as they create drag in the water, but it is all so intensely quiet and peaceful. You principally hear leaves rustling from the breeze on shore and birds chirping by the thousands. We have moved, in a matter of a minute, from a cacophony to comparative silence.

Except that we talk. But we talk in an environment where suddenly you can hear yourself think. We laugh and joke. Ty asks Livie if she remembered our big bottle of hand sanitizer. Livie wonders which is more important: hand sanitizer or a life jacket? Not missing a beat, I say:

"There's a decision that would completely paralyze your mother."

Oh, the laughs. And we are off.

---

OUR OARSMAN IS NOT EXACTLY an expert. But he is certainly more an expert than I. He once took kayaking lessons and has spent many more hours on river water than I have, whether on a kayak, raft, or inner tube.

I first met Ty Rosean about a decade ago. I had finished my postgraduate studies in Aberdeen, Scotland, and we had finally made the pilgrimage home to Billings. One of our first Sundays back at our church Ty happened to be visiting with his girlfriend, and I remember they had three children with them. It turned out they were babysitting one or two of them. There was a visitor's lunch after the service and since we were kind of, sort of new we stuck around. So did they.

The first thing that struck me is that Ty is a talker. A very easy talker. I don't know if you've ever noticed, but the vast majority of people have a certain level of awkwardness talking to strangers for the first time. Ty speaks with casual, confident assurance, completely comfortable in his own skin. I ask him to introduce me to his wife, and he laughs and tells me he doesn't have a wife. She is his girlfriend and they've been living together for eight years. And he's only the father of one of their two kids. It was kind of refreshing to hear somebody talk so freely like this in a church. I mean, in a church setting people are usually more hesitant to say, "I'm fornicating with my girlfriend who has also had somebody else's baby." I remember being kind of impressed.

Ty was not a Christian. Or maybe he kind of thought he was, the way lots of Joe Sixpack Americans think they're Christians. But his girlfriend had reconnected with a friend who attended our church, so Ty tagged along, I think, partly to irritate her. So he showed up one Sunday and never left. That's barely a figure of speech. He hangs around the church office like the staff pet, hoping to gain wisdom from the pastors by osmosis or something. He met Jesus along the way and experienced the excruciating joys of a life renovation. The relationship went south and she went on to have another child with yet another father. Having journeyed with Ty through the mess for a decade, I cannot recommend promiscuity as a family formation strategy. And believe me, with constant struggles of co-parenting his son, neither does he.

Some would call Ty a layabout. He doesn't seem to work very often. He runs a merchant services business, which basically means he helps businesses large and small set up and navigate the murky world of credit card processing. His portfolio provides him a decent passive residual income and a whole lot of time on his hands. At 36, with no college degree, Ty is always wondering what he is going to be when he grows up. I have a plan for his life, and have to remind him of it often.

Ty Rosean isn't really a layabout. Yes, he doesn't punch a time clock or spend a ton of time doing the kind of salesmanship his industry generally expects (mostly they expect the slimy, shady kind). What he does do is serve people. Constantly. One day he's helping friends drywall their basement. The next he's running electrical wire for somebody else. Installing a ceiling fan for somebody infirm. All volunteer, any time, day or night, if you need help with anything at all, there is one person you call. Every church service project, there's one guy you can count on to be there. I have never known him not to drop everything at a request for help. It really helps that he is handy with tools. In my case, it's handy that he *has* tools—after all these years he's still laughing at me for not having a cordless drill. I try to encourage him to see that this is, in fact, his calling. God has given him a passive income precisely so that he can serve all of these people. I don't think there are many 36 year olds who would fill that kind of free time with just blessing other people.

I don't actually remember becoming friends, and that's the best kind of friendship. It happens so organically there is never a moment where the thought occurs to you: "Now we are friends." Somehow Ty was woven into the fabric of our lives without us ever realizing it. He drops by randomly and eats dinner with us regularly, always generously supplying copious amounts of wine for the occasion.

Ty is amazing with children. All three of his "kids" call him Dad, even though it is only true of one of them and the other two never live with him anymore. When Baby-Daddy Number Three shockingly committed suicide right after a visitation with his young daughter, Ty took care of that baby like she was his own. Ty is so fatherly that I swear one time even one of my own children called him "Dad." She's scheduled to be unchained from the basement water heater next month. I kid.

Organic friendships are hard to come by, and so I give thanks for those I have. I struggle, actually, to think in terms of "what we have in common." What a ridiculous standard for relationships, if you think about it. Who really wants uniformity? Yes, we like single malt whisky and baseball, and probably lots of other things. But they are utterly secondary. Somehow, some way, we just started caring about each other.

*"One who has unreliable friends soon comes to ruin; but there is a friend that sticks closer than a brother."*

— Proverbs 18:24

4

# ON ANGLING

"O Sir, doubt not that Angling is an art; is it not an art to deceive a Trout with an artificial Fly? a Trout! that is more sharp-sighted than any Hawk you have named, and more watchful and timorous than your high-mettled Merlin is bold? and yet, I doubt not to catch a brace or two to-morrow, for a friend's breakfast: doubt not, therefore, Sir, but that angling is an art, and an art worth your learning."

— Isaak Walton, The Compleat Angler

We float for quite a long time before I decide to put my fly rod to use. I am probably missing out on some good water, but we need to get our "sea legs." I want Ty to get acclimated to maneuvering the vessel before I start whipping flies all around the boat. Besides, the water looks murky to me, and I want to just look at it, analyze it, and decide what sort of fly I should try. After awhile I realize that I can actually see rocks on the river bottom, which is the only clue I really need. Fish can see far better than we give them credit for, and many an angler has made the mistake of prematurely giving up on "muddy" waters.

I must make a customary excursus here. I am a Montanan, born and raised, and I am a fly fisherman, and those two things combined have almost religious significance in my part of the world, as Norman MacLean canonically decreed for all time. Fly fishing involves a lot of science—the gear, the materials of graphite, monofilament nylon, and brass hooks wound with a variety of animal hair. One may study hydrology and the movement of water around rocks and other obstacles, study the physics of launching a fly practically lighter than air through rough winds and to land it softly near the opposite shore. And then there's entomology, the life courses of a vast variety of insects in their larvae, pupa, and adult forms. Too many are misled by all this.

Fly fishing is art.

---

BAIT FISHING USES "ARTIFICIAL" attractants. Pull a big, spinning, shiny object through water and fish will usually bite it out of pure curiosity. Alternatively, put something juicy and smelly on a hook like an earthworm and it arguably isn't even fair play. Bait is something abnormal for a fish; they attack it for its novelty.

The art of fly fishing is to fabricate a purely synthetic insect and manipulate it through the water (either under the water, "nymph fishing," or on top of the water, "dry fly fishing") so that a fish doesn't give it a second thought, wholly convinced it is their perfectly normal food supply. The trickery, the con, is much more subtle and much more difficult than bait fishing; Daniel Day-Lewis style, one must always be "in character."

I am inexpert at this, having taken up the sport only eight years ago. Rather shameful for a lifelong Montanan, but better late than never. For this year's birthday I was able to purchase a lot of new gear; up until now I have been using a lot of hand-me-down equipment my Dad gave me when he became so exasperated by fly fishing that he quit. I now sport proper wading pants and boots, and a gold-plated fishing vest with more pockets than craters on the moon. Now I fish while looking like a walking Simms commercial, and I don't know how I feel about that. I don't like being cliché, but truthfully all this equipment really is useful and not just for show.

Now I am fishing from a raft, which is much easier, technique-wise, than fishing from shore. While on shore, the fisherman must cast his line upstream and obtain a lengthy "dead drift" without the line dragging the fly unnaturally, all the while ensuring there is not too much slack in the line. It is irritating, to say the least, to have a fish take your fly and you cannot set the hook because you're pulling slack instead of the fly. On a raft, all this becomes far easier because you are already drifting with the water. Toss the fly in, and it's inherently a "dead drift."

You still need to know where the fish are, and this is a skill developed with long experience. Someone can tell you theoretically how to "read" water, but it is no substitute for actually seeing it and putting it into practice. Often there is a seam of quiet water right next to fast water; drift your fly right along that seam. Fish don't like to fight a current all day. They hang out in the calm and dart in to the current when they see food floating by.

Often there are "shelves" in the water, when the river bottom drops suddenly and riffles spill into a deep pool. Fish love to sit below the shelf and watch bugs emerge over their heads. Rocks and obstacles, of which there are many in the Smith River, are also classic fish hideouts, only not where many fishermen think. It is natural to assume that fish are hiding directly behind the rock in the calm water, and from time to time you might catch one there. But more commonly, believe it or not, a trout will sit tight right *in front* of the rock. The alternative is to fish the "tail" of the hole, the V-shaped spot where the two currents created by the obstacle reunite. This requires a very good drift because the fish will see the fly for a long time, veering around the rock toward the tail. One flick, one bump, one tiny drag against the current and the fly will look unnatural and you will be out of luck. Make a habit of it, and you'll get skunked and catch nothing all day. Ninety percent of fly fishing is proper presentation of the fly. If you're not catching anything, don't assume it is the temperature or time of day or lack of cloud cover or choice of fly or size of fly or moon cycles or any other ingenious, self-serving lies fishermen tell themselves. The problem, nine times out of ten, is the fisherman. It is humbling, but only the truth will set us free.

A lot of fly fishermen are hopelessly distracted by entomology, thinking that they must match the perfect fly (and perfect size!) to the exact insect hatch at exactly the right time of year. In broad strokes, that might be true; you don't really want to be fishing with a stone fly if stone flies are completely out of season, or, say, using grasshoppers in April. But mostly "matching" insects is only relevant at a very specific time—a hatch is occurring right before your eyes and the water is boiling with trout rising to the surface. Which doesn't happen that often.

I actually believe—and since I'm not a great angler, feel free to disregard it—a fisherman only really needs a half a dozen good flies, since many of them do double and triple duty along the spectrum of entomological variations. There are a lot of flies that are, quite simply, good enough for the job. If it looks like real food and is presented properly, a trout will eat it. It really is that simple, and there is no need to overcomplicate an already complicated task.

On this day, I try a number of things. I've researched fishing reports on the Smith River, and have discovered that the waters are very similar to what I normally fish. I rig a two fly system, with the second fly a foot below the first on the line. One of these two flies will, for the duration, be my old standby, the fly that never disappoints: the bead-headed Prince Nymph, with its V-shaped signature white wings. If there is such a thing as a trout menu, I think the Prince Nymph is the chocolate lava cake. At least in the streams I fish.

The fishing is slow with not a lot of action, but on this day I catch three, one of each of the most common species in the Smith: a Rainbow Trout, a Brown Trout, and a rather large Whitefish. Olivia catches two Rainbows herself, making me proud. The Whitefish I hook just as we are heading toward a cliff wall. Ty is heaving the oars, spinning the raft around, the waters are rough. I've got my net in my left hand and my rod in my right. I scoop the fish out of the water and duck out of the way just as the cliff face scrapes the starboard side of the raft. Just in time.

---

A WORD about these species of fish. The Whitefish, until just a few years ago, was not considered a game fish in

Montana. It is a bottom-feeder with a tiny little puckered mouth. Their skeletal structure makes filleting this fish very burdensome. But enough people keep them (and typically dry them out in a smoker) that they are now regulated as a game fish. I do not much care for Whitefish. When hooked, they never dazzle you with aerial acrobatics the way trout do. They stay under the water and resist, and you get the feeling you are just dragging a log, as if the creature is reluctantly saying, "Okay, you caught me." You wouldn't think it to look at them, but they are also astonishingly fragile fish for their heft. If you take longer than a few moments to remove the hook from their mouths, when you place them back in the water they will immediately go belly up. You must point their faces into the current so the water flows over the gills, and gently hold them upright until—and this may take awhile—with a startled jolt they kick themselves out of shock and flee your presence.

The Rainbow Trout is the Ferrari—fast and agile beyond belief. They will soar into the air to create enough slack to escape the hook. They are fighters and a joy to catch. They have a reputation of being beautiful fish, with their rainbow-like stripe on their silvery flanks, as well as being good eating. They are in high demand at fancy restaurants, and I think it has more to do with their pleasant good-looks than it does better flavor.

For me, the prize is the Brown Trout. What an ugly, terrible, no-good name. The Brown is not, as its boring moniker would lead you to believe, "brown." I believe they are the most beautiful of all trout (with the possible exception of the Brook): flecks of brown, green, amber, gold, blue, with bright symmetrically placed red spots. From the vantage point of a Bald Eagle, they are nothing more than moving and writhing river rocks. From below, they match the pale, off-white blue of the sky and clouds. Aircraft painters in World War II must have taken their cue from these creatures.

Browns are aggressive carnivores and grow into very large, powerful fish. Hook a Brown, and you will have the fight of your life on your hands. Be prepared for all kinds of hijinks: bolting for exposed rocks or deadfall that will tangle your line, or beelining straight upstream into rapids. Once I hooked a Brown in the middle of a deep pool. I knew I had hooked a fish, but since he did not come out of the water, I couldn't tell what kind. Well, this wily old fellow dove straight to the bottom of the hole and just sat there. For a very long time. So long I started to wonder if perhaps I wasn't mistaken and had simply snagged my line on something inanimate. I tugged a little, and felt the tell-tale tug, tug in return. Rocks do not tug. Suddenly, like a fighter jet in a full-afterburner vertical takeoff, the Brown shot from the depths straight up and out of the pool, at least five feet over the surface, twisting and shaking beads of water everywhere, like jewels scattering in the sunlight. Like Icarus, he fell from the sky and eventually made his way into my net.

Reverend MacLean would have remarked, "Just beautiful."

There are those who will no doubt tell me that these perfectly camouflaged fish are the end result of the mere mechanisms of a long line of biological evolution. But when I stand in a river bathed in late afternoon Autumn sunlight, with diamond beads of water sparkling off my line, the leaves around me green and amber, gold and red, the river rocks pale, and the sky brilliant blue—when I catch a fish who happens to be green and amber, gold and red, pale, and blue, I see an Artist at work. I am looking at one of his many signature styles.

> *"Blessed are your eyes because they see, and your ears because they hear."*
>
> — MATTHEW 13:16

---

THE MACLEAN BOYS would no doubt be disappointed in me. They amusingly thought that being a dry fly fisherman meant that one was closer to Jesus. Here I am, a theologian by vocation, and I am not a good dry fly fisherman. Hopefully I still rank above their utterly despised "bait fishermen" who take an empty coffee can out to the garden to dig up worms. But dry flies are an infuriating art all their own. The trouble is that you are essentially trying to float a tiny, delicate feather on moving waters. A "dry" fly never stays dry. It gets wet and soggy and has a natural concupiscence to sink below the surface—there's a spiritual lesson there somewhere. Human beings as dry flies, fallen from grace, always bent to sink lower. And to complete the metaphor, I guess: devoured.

As you can surmise, the object is to float the fly on the surface. When it works, there is no greater thrill in all the world of fishing because the trout rises out of the water to take the fly. It happens so suddenly, in so spontaneously joyous a moment, that one often flinches in delight and is late setting the hook—or one forgets altogether. The trout just spits it out once he has the rude realization that he must have made some kind of mistake.

Casting dries is a real challenge because one must land them on the surface in just such a way as to not have too much slack in the line. Trying to fiddle with slack or "mend" the line while the fly is on the water is—at least for me—hopeless. One move of the rod and the fly sadly slinks into the depths. There are some substances you can buy to help waterproof the fly, gooey stuff called "gink," which is a perfect name as it calls to mind "gunk" and "ick." It doesn't really work for me anyway.

Fly fishing sounds like so monumental a hassle you might wonder why anyone would bother with it. And I haven't even attempted to explain how confounding a tangle a fly rod can cause when not cast properly. The truth is that it is a monumental hassle, from the expense of the gear to the technicalities of execution. Legion is the number of people, like my father, who simply give up. But something happens that is magical. One day you'll be fishing and suddenly realize that you are not thinking about fishing. You have not, in fact, been concentrating on your casting rhythm or mending your line in the water properly. You have simply been fishing. Handling the rod has become an autonomous muscle reflex. You are putting the fly exactly where you want it on the water without conscious thought. A strange feeling of oneness with the river and its rhythms comes over you. It is no wonder at all to me that people interpret this in mystical terms, as did MacLean, and, more recently David James Duncan in his 1983 novel, *The River Why*.

It is oneness with the river, but not in a pagan sense of some kind of shared being or essence. It is oneness in the sense of "belonging together." A human skillfully handling a fly rod is exercising his or her native charter to wield dominion over the fish of the sea. When "chief ends" are being performed, whether with conscious purpose or not, it cannot help but be a thrill of exhilaration. Scottish Olympian Eric Liddell once said, "When I run, I feel God's pleasure." That is the feeling, as well as the reason for the feeling.

---

THE SECOND DAY of our float ends with a scene of otherworldly beauty in my mind, like heaven had arrived early. I stand in a dark river facing an imposing gray cliff. Mist rises slowly from the water and gray clouds hang low. Swallows dart in and out of their nests in the eaves. The slow, deep water at the foot of the cliff is rippled by concentric rings. The swallows are not the only ones feeding on this bounteous hatch. In the past I've wondered about Norman MacLean's lovely phrase, "the Arctic half-light of the canyon," but I am now standing in it and I know why he added no explanation. It can only be experienced.

As the water roils in front of me, I patiently tie on a dry. In a rhythmic four-count, I cast the fly back and forth, further distant and further distant, and finally land my tiny speck on the black surface just underneath the eave of the cliff. A splash, shock and surprise, it disappears in a swirl of water. Instinctively I pull back on the rod firmly and feel it catch. For a moment.

I am tardy. And I am blessed.

I feel His pleasure.

## 5

## CLIFF JUMPER

"True hope is swift, and flies with swallow's wings;
Kings it makes gods, and meaner creatures kings."

— Shakespeare, Richard III 5.2

It is late afternoon our first day. The light fades and the canyon darkens. For the first time I notice something spectacular. Camouflaged against the sides of the gray ravine are nests full of cliff swallows. Not a dozen nests, not hundreds, but thousands of them. Perfect, tiny little homes aligned in rows with perfect, tiny holes in front, all tucked perfectly under rock ledges. The swallows have been darting around the river all day, but it hasn't occurred to me to really pay attention to where they're coming from.

I watch carefully, and I see a small avian head peek out from a hole. The swallow leaps out, a champion cliff jumper, hurling straight down toward the water. She explodes to her left, and then to her right as her wings spread, catch, and expertly manipulate the air. Effortlessly, she changes directions on a dime, sometimes 180 degrees at full speed. It seems like an illusion, as she moves so quickly my eyes can barely track her. She and hundreds of her friends are now diving around the raft, swooping by us—within our reach, if only we were quick enough. I begin counting how many swallows emerge from a single nest, and it reminds me of that circus trick where clowns keep getting out of the Volkswagen. Those nests are a lot more roomy than they seem. All of the birds seem to be coming out to play with us.

But we are actually quite incidental to their purpose. Insects are hatching, probably mayflies or caddis. Underneath the water they are crawling out of their eggs and swimming for the surface, where they emerge with newfound wings that many of them will use only long enough to make it to the mouth of a ravenous swallow. A very short lifespan that serves God's good purpose.

> *"Look at the birds of the air; they do not sow or reap or store away in barns, and yet your heavenly Father feeds them. Are you not much more valuable than they?"*
>
> — Matthew 6:26

---

The Smith meanders out of Camp Baker for a mile or two before it turns into a slinky. Hairpin turns pile up on each other as the water plunges into the canyon, and it only evens out, we discover, on the other end some fifty miles ahead. The turns are a challenge. At the start of the journey, loaded down with weight, our raft is sluggish in the water and as we approach the bends the water seems determined to dash us against the opposing rock wall. It's tricky business getting the raft facing just the right way to avoid this. We are in the school of hard knocks—literally. Three or four times we cannot quite avoid hitting the cliff, ducking our heads from dangerous overhangs.

The rock walls are not our only hazard. We discover that this time of year the water level is down and there are a lot of large rocks just barely submerged in the water. This means two problems: they are very difficult to see until we are almost right on top of them, leaving *Titanic*-like time to maneuver. As in, no time at all. The rocks are so close to the surface that when we hit them they can stop the raft cold. Alternatively, if we manage to clip a rock just a bit off-center, it spins the raft wildly. We're not terribly worried about puncturing the raft—these vessels are very sturdy. We're more concerned about getting dumped into the river when the raft suddenly stops.

We have good reason to be concerned, as it turns out.

Another rafter had told me that the Smith River is a "postcard around every bend," and I am finding this to be true. In the early afternoon I have my phone out to take pictures. Ty thinks that's a great idea, so I offer to take the oars for awhile so he can sit in the bow, enjoy the view, and take some photos himself. He digs his phone out of a dry bag to capture a scene or two. The phone somehow finds its way back into his pocket instead of the dry bag.

It appears so suddenly. The massive rock causes barely a ripple on the surface, and by the time I see it we have no chance to miss it. "Rock!" I yell, a mere instant before the side of the raft meets it. The raft slams to a halt, but Ty does not. I see him caught off balance and fly straight over the side. He hits the river flat on his back and I see the waters completely consume him, head to toe. He bounces straight back up, grabbing the side rope, scrambling over into the boat, thankfully laughing.

Only after catching his breath for a few minutes and rebuffing my moaning apologies, he realizes what he's done. He pulls his iPhone out of his soggy pocket, but it shows nothing but the black screen of death. Our first casualty.

The rest of our company has an equal, if not more difficult, time. All day as we look back we see our companions with their rafts hung up on rocks or sandbars, or slamming into canyon walls. We feel a bit better, knowing we are not the only ones having a hard time with this learning curve—or should I say the canyon is throwing us learning *curves*?

At lunchtime we all stop at a U.S. Forest Service boat camp, our first glimpse of these primitive outposts. Boat camps have some common features. Heavy posts are stuck in the ground fairly high on shore so that one can tie up a raft well out of the river in case of a sudden rise in water level. A small, helpful sign has an arrow pointing to the "latrine," along with a trail leading to it. At this camp the latrine is on the top of a hill. It is very disconcerting sitting on a toilet in the open air looking down on the river and being able to see people. I have no idea what possessed somebody to place it there, but in truth it feels more exposed than it actually is. I can say it is the most beautiful spot to relieve oneself I've ever seen.

Nancy has brought giant ziplock bags full of cold, fried chicken. She insists we eat some, along with the sandwiches we've brought. It is delicious, as is the accompanying can of ice-cold Rainier beer.

---

I JUST FELT the reader's eyes narrow again, an eyebrow raised, the heat of harsh judgment. I imagine there are two kinds of fundamentalists reading this: The teetotaling kind, and the non-teetotaling kind.

The first read that sentence and thought, *"Beer!? How dare he?"*

The second read that sentence and thought, "*Rainier!? How dare he?*"

A word to both. Contrary to conventional wisdom, teetotaling and Christianity do not fit very comfortably together. That this image endures in popular imagination has more to do with recent American sociology than anything related to the Bible or 2,000 years of Christian tradition. Christians for centuries the world over have, along with everyone else, crafted and enjoyed alcoholic beverages. The now-dominant American fundamentalist streak is an early 20th century phenomenon, a largely political movement with the dubious distinction of passing the disastrous social and economic experiment known as "Prohibition." When it comes to history, teetotaling is the *novel* interpretation of what the Bible teaches.

And it is incorrect. The Bible says a lot about alcohol abuse, but that is precisely the meaningful distinction: use versus *abuse*. The *stuff* is not the problem; *abusing* the stuff is the problem. The Bible also says a lot about gluttony, and nobody thinks the solution is to stop eating. And let's get real about something: for most of human history, people have known that drinking water can kill you. Yes, they didn't know about bacteria *per se*, but they knew that water can be deadly. So they regularly and wisely drank fermented things—even strict religious people! When the separatists known as the "Pilgrims" (as religiously strict a group as you can imagine) were preparing to board the *Mayflower* for their transatlantic voyage, do you know one of the top things they worried about? Whether they'd have enough beer for the journey. They didn't *dare* drink water on that trip. Teetotaling, you see, is something of a luxury of the modern world, with our newfangled water purification techniques; in previous times, you purified water by making beer, wine, or spirits with it. If you did drink water, it was from a well that you knew—or had every reason to believe—was uncontaminated.

Now to the "other" kind of fundamentalist—or "purist," if you prefer. Rainier? *Rainier*? In this day and age, with thousands of microbreweries that make real beer, why am I drinking a weak industrial American lager out of a can? I mean, I'm not a hipster, but I've been accused occasionally of looking like one. I am generally known for appreciating the finer things: single malt scotch, for example. I credit Ty—credit, not *blame*—for converting me to the wonders of what we call "Vitamin R."

It began a few summers back during fireworks "season." That's what we call the two weeks before the 4th of July, because Ty manages a fireworks stand each year up in Columbus, Montana. He takes a camper to a small lot right next to the highway and lives there with his dog Foster, a plucky miniature Australian Shepherd with one brilliant blue eye and one dark brown. I've got in the habit of going up to visit Ty for a couple of days during this time, mostly because it's already close to my normal fly fishing spots, but also because he's since started hiring Olivia and her friend Grace to help him those weeks.

The first time I ever visited, Ty asked: "Want a Vitamin R?"

I had no idea what he was talking about, so I asked for clarification.

"Rainier."

All of my latent snobbery emerged. He insisted that I did not know what I was talking about and that Rainier is the best of the big lagers—way better than Budweiser or Coors or Miller. I may be a snob, and I was certainly skeptical, but I also like to try new things. So, of course, I accepted a can of Rainier.

On that blazing hot June afternoon, fresh from fishing the Stillwater River, that cold beer hit my palate at the perfect time. I could hardly disagree. I enjoyed that Rainier far more than any other of the "big" beers I'd had. Maybe that isn't saying much. The big industrial canned beers are not to be compared with the microbrew revolution, but I still maintain that there is a time and place for them. While I wouldn't drink it on a regular basis, I've come to associate Vitamin R with Ty Rosean, Walt Longmire, and summertime. Walt Longmire is a fictional character in a television show, but I am now on the Smith River with Ty Rosean in June. Two out of three ain't bad. So we've got plenty of Vitamin R.

He provides for the swallows, and he provides for us.

. . .

NOTE: *A party stunt that always gets a huge laugh is to read aloud the italicized verbiage on the side of a Budweiser can. I don't want to be hearing from the lawyers of Anheiser-Busch, so I won't spoil it for you here. Just do it some time. You'll find that it isn't exactly "truth in advertising."*

---

WE'VE PLANNED it so that our first day floating is also our longest day. We're traveling twenty miles downriver, and it turns out that is a very long distance. But it is also plenty of time to get the hang of maneuvering the river. I am grateful that Ty decides he really likes handling the oars, because I don't. He's probably just saying that to be polite; it's equally likely that he distrusts my rafting abilities after unceremoniously dumping him and his iPhone in the river. At any rate, he takes charge of navigating, which allows Livie and I ample time to fish.

We have a very useful river map provided by the Forest Service that marks every bend of the river and every boat camp. The trouble is, on this first day, we are not heading for a boat camp. We are looking for a private cabin owned by some friends of Royal and Nancy. The fifty-nine mile stretch of the Smith River is remote and not publicly accessible, but frequently private property and cabins appear on the shores. Someone in our party has marked with a Sharpie an "X" the approximate spot on the map for our searched-for settlement, but this is definitely more guesswork than a camp would be. The sun is getting low and we are sailing in shadow. Around every bend we increasingly wonder if we've already passed our destination. Royal's raft is ahead of us, and several times we shout to him asking if he's sure we're on the right track. He assures us that it's just around the next bend.

It takes a few more bends.

At last, as we swing around a starboard turn, we see a sight for sore eyes. A beautiful cabin sits back a hundred yards from the shore. Smoke rises from a grill on a large, sweeping deck. A figure rises from a seat and starts waving. It seems our arrival has been anticipated, after all.

We pull to the port side onto a gravel bar and tie up the raft. A white pickup truck approaches down the drive and a face familiar to many of our company steps out. Paul Robinson emerges with cold beers all around, inviting us to throw all of our gear in the truck bed for transport up to the cabin. This begins our red carpet treatment.

It takes a few minutes to get our "land legs" back. The whole earth seems to undulate and slosh from side to side. It is like the rocking of the raft has imprinted itself on our brains—"inner ear" is probably more technically true. The feeling subsides a bit as we walk up to the "cabin," which turns out to be a euphemism for "really spectacular house on a beautiful river." The deck is massive, filled with plush outdoor furniture and an outdoor gas fireplace, directly overlooking the river and the giant gray cliffs looming over the far shore. Paul's lovely wife Betty shows us a bathroom where we can get cleaned up. Their 18-year-old son Sean appears—he has been happily setting up half a dozen air mattresses upstairs. I am astonished, having expected that we would set up our tent in the yard. But they have planned for everybody to sleep indoors.

I am pointed to a old retro-looking refrigerator in the garage which, Betty slyly tells me, contains the "real" beer. I check it out and am astonished. Not only are the bottles ice cold, there are dozens and dozens of them. Packed to the brim with every conceivable kind. I'm a guy stranded in the desert who discovers the mirage actually is an oasis.

Dinner follows. That smoking grill? It holds sections of massive seasoned beef tenderloins, four or five of them. Multiple salads, mashed potatoes, corn on the cob, and bottles of expensive Zinfandel complete the feast.

The Lord does not just provide for cliff swallows. He provides us with Paul and Betty Robinson of Great Falls, Montana.

THEIR SON, SEAN, IS A "LOOKER." A turn-the-head, "wonder-if-he's-an-Abercrombie-model" sort of handsome. Confident, self-assured, the high school senior makes an immediate good impression by having the knack (sadly, rather unusual for the age) of being able to have winsome and intelligent conversations with adults. I also marvel how he routinely asks his mother what he can do to help. When the night ends, he stays up late doing dishes and taking out trash.

Olivia notices him, I can tell. I mean, he is the kind of young man that is difficult for a young lady to miss. Of course, as is my fatherly prerogative, I tease her mercilessly later. It turns out that since she's the only one anywhere close to his age in our traveling party, he notices her, too.

He kindly asks her after dinner if she would like to jump off a cliff.

Yes, jump off a cliff.

I had always thought the old parenting adage was hyperbole: "If your friends told you to jump off a cliff, would you?" But here he is, asking her to jump off a cliff, and she is eagerly saying, "Yes!"

He politely asks me, too, but the answer is an automatic, "No, thank you." I hate heights, and it is getting cold as the sun is far away from our darkening canyon. But Olivia is eager, perhaps because a cute boy asked her, perhaps because she's a budding thrill-seeker, but I think most probably because Betty tells her that cliff jumpers get to use the hot shower afterward.

A small company of us set off through what turns out to be a subdivision of cabins on the Smith River. I can see my breath in the now-dim light. Sean explains that this swimming hole—a deep bend in the river—has been used for decades by families in this neighborhood, and he assures me that nobody has ever even felt the bottom after jumping off the cliff. That makes me feel better, but I am still glad that Olivia's mother is not here. Our pact is: "What happens on the Smith stays on the Smith."

Until Dad writes a book about it, that is.

We arrive at a green lawn on the riverbank. Across the river, the cliff appears massive. Sean did not mention that one first has to swim across the river, *then* climb the other side while shivering and dripping wet. He also didn't mention that one practically must be an expert rock climber to accomplish the second task. Olivia is undeterred, and the two of them swim across. It looks positively freezing.

Sean climbs like a mountain goat up the rock face, and then verbally guides Olivia: "Okay. Reach your right hand up to the right, and put your left foot up and to the left" sort of instructions. To my amazement, she makes it to the ledge on which he's standing without losing her grip and being forced to push herself away from the cliff into the water—a half-expected outcome.

From my vantage point, they are specks in the middle of a giant limestone slate with deep, black water at the base. They are twenty-five feet up, which is considered the low platform. That may not seem high, but you have to see it to get a real feel for how terrifying it is. A tiny bush pokes out from the wall at thirty-five feet, which is the high platform Olivia has wisely declined to try.

I can hear them talking for awhile, just standing there. Sean is giving instructions and offering encouragement. I catch a bit of it. The most important thing, he says, is to push away from the cliff far enough to avoid the small lip at the bottom that juts out into the water. Again, I am so glad her mother isn't here.

Finally, Sean leaps from the ledge and plunges into the water. Everybody cheers.

Olivia stands alone.

---

SHE HAS ALWAYS BEEN what you would call a risk-averse child. Tara and I have sat at countless parks and playgrounds in her lifetime—in Billings, inner-city Philadelphia, northeast Scotland. Parents the world over are always jumping up from their benches to run to the aid of their children who climb or swing a little bit too high for comfort. To our recollection, we've never left our seats. She was meticulous and careful in every way, never clumsy. Her younger sister turned out to be—as we called it—"almost clumsy," and our family DNA has, at long last, finally devolved to the point where our youngest is actually clumsy.

But never Olivia. Combined with her excellent sense of danger was her incredible toughness. Of course, in some ways we trained her to be tough. We've never been ones to immediately run to the rescue of a child who falls and skins a knee or bumps their head. We always encouraged her to just dust herself off and keep moving. She was uncannily compliant. On the very rare occasions when she did fall or bang her head, she would immediately leap up and yell, "I'm okay!" We far preferred this reaction to the much-more-ordinary bawling. In addition to providing pleasant, drama-free parenting, this philosophy has the perk of revealing when our children really need assistance: if they cry, they're truly hurt. I can remember few occasions when tears were involved. But, as I say, Olivia has always lived on the conservative side of life.

---

I AM SITTING on a chair at the shore of a deep Montana river at twilight and my firstborn baby is standing alone high above. I envision her rapid breathing, but I am too distant to see her breath. There is no one to help and there is no way down except adopting the way of a wingless cliff swallow.

At last, she takes a deep breath and leaps.

As she plummets into the depths and reemerges a moment later, my fatherly heart bursts with the strange sensation of melancholy pride.

She has wings, after all.

## 6

# HAILSTORM & FIREWATER

> "Yet it is opportune that a voice be raised in defence of this great, potent, and princely drink where so many speak to slight and defame, and where so many glasses are emptied foolishly and irreverently in ignorance of the true qualities of the liquid and in contempt of its proper employment."
>
> — Aeneas MacDonald, Whisky

The smell of coffee and bacon wafts up the stairs to the common room where we've slept comfortably on our air mattresses. I hear the chatter of the older people below. They've been up for awhile and, as men and women of mature age do, they are talking about the weather. Today it isn't just the usual small talk.

The forecast from the start of the journey was that on

this day a storm front is moving in. The weather app on my phone had promised me that it will begin raining at 3 o'clock in the afternoon, and continue steadily through the night and all the way through the next day. It does sound miserable.

The decision is a difficult one. The Smith River has no public access, which means that once you are in the river, there is no getting out. There is this single exception: you might happen to know a private landowner who is willing to let you off the river. And Paul and Betty are more than willing to help arrange rides back to Camp Baker for anyone who decides that memories of one beautiful day on the river shouldn't be sullied with two or three cold and wet days after.

Unsurprisingly, this happens to be a popular view in our expeditionary party, especially as a few of our company have discovered a defective dry bag resulting in a couple of wet sleeping bags. Calls and arrangements are made from a Sat-phone, and one by one our group decides to disband. Ty, Olivia, and I have to make a decision. On the one hand, we do want to continue the journey. This is a once-in-a-lifetime trip, and we do not want to live with the "what ifs" involved in not persevering. On the other hand, we know that we are very inexperienced. Is it responsible to strike out completely on our own?

Bill and Betty Black come to our rescue. These two hardy Montanans are not put off by a little inclement weather, and they decide they'd like to continue on, so long as we are going, too. So the decision is made. For the sake of adventure, we will float on, rain or shine.

---

Bill Black is a living, breathing, walking, and talking Herman Melville character. He is exactly like you'd imagine a sailor in *Moby Dick* to look. He has a leathery, wrinkled face, and a white beard. His eyes give off a twinkle of good humor, which is no deception. He is terrifically funny. The only mode of humor he knows is sarcasm, and he's had a lifetime to perfect the art. He is without a doubt the single-most sarcastic cuss I've ever met. He is also incredibly helpful and experienced; this is not his first time down the Smith River. I get the impression that in ancient days, before the river was a permit-only affair, he did this trip many times. At least, I figure out that he knows the names and locations of every single boat camp without the aid of a map. As it turns out, he's on a first-name basis with just about every Forest Service Ranger, too.

Bill is surprisingly strong and agile, which disguises the fact that after decades of hard labor his body is breaking down with arthritic aches and pains. It also disguises the effects of the rather unique medication he uses for his various afflictions, which is strictly over-the-counter and comparatively inexpensive. It's called Bacardi 151, affectionately known as "151." The number is important because, in adult beverage terms, it is the "proof" of this particular bottling of rum. "151" means that this firewater is over 75 percent alcohol, whereas ordinary rum is bottled at 40. This basically means it could tranquilize an elephant, if you could just get an elephant to drink it.

He keeps the 151 in a sizeable plastic bottle, I can only presume because an ordinary flask is wholly insufficient to the quantities needed. He takes frequent, man-sized pulls of the stuff without a grimace, which I find impressive. He's like an outlaw in a western, only he doesn't like whiskey or rye. I offer him a taste of our smoky single malt from time to time, and he gruffly rebuffs me. He's a rum guy, through and through.

This adds to the Melville mystique, but even more so does his raft. Bill and Betty are floating on a two-person vessel called a *Boston Whaler*. He sits low in the stern with the oars, and Betty sits on a seat high in front of him midship. It is a very agile raft because of its size. The oars take a sharp angle down to the water, and one look at him paddling away and I can't help but think of Captain Ahab setting out to harpoon a white whale.

---

So we are down to five souls in two vessels. After a full breakfast—bacon and coffee is always a perfect combination—we push off the gravel bar from the Robinsons, generously stocked with all the leftover tenderloin and mashed potatoes from the night before. As we head into the middle of the river, I feel compelled to say a prayer out loud. It is a simple one, thanking God for our wonderful trip so far, the amazing hospitality of our hosts, and then I get very specific: "God, please let us get to our camp today before the rain begins."

Bill and Betty are out of earshot, but later when I tell Bill my prayer, his rather cynical reply reminds me of someone else: Puddleglum the Marshwiggle, from C.S. Lewis's *The Silver Chair*. There is simply no state of affairs about which Bill Black cannot immediately find the downside. He identifies dark linings in every silver cloud. If you tell him the sun is going to shine, he'll say you're damned certain to get sunburned or dehydrated—in fact, you'll get burned to a crisp and likely won't last the day. We discover that the act is downright charming—another thing he has in common with Puddleglum. Olivia likes him, I suspect partly because she is getting an education in salty language. He looks like a sailor in his *Boston Whaler*, and he matches it with his mouth.

The sun does shine and the day is fair, and we are motivated to make the most of it before the storm inevitably hits. Livie and I fish some more, though the water is even muddier today and we have no luck. Tired of just watching her strike indicator float along without a bite, she reels it in and sets her rod off to the side.

This turns out to be a mistake. Ty is getting quite good

at handling the sharp turns, but the raft gets away from him once and we crash into a cliff. A few moments later we notice something odd: her fluorescent fishing line is dragging behind the raft. She pulls it in, and the top section of her fly rod is severed in half; it has smashed on a rock overhang. Another piece of equipment joins Ty's iPhone in our list of casualties—actually, believe it or not, the iPhone is showing more signs of life than the fly rod. Betty had put it in a bowl of rice overnight, and the screen now at least flickers.

The power of moving water constantly amazes us. I have no idea why we are so amazed; after all, this liquid carved our path 59 miles straight through solid limestone. Nevertheless, I have a bright idea that almost gets us killed. I spy a place up ahead where the river has chiseled a dark cave right into the rock. The waters form a little cove and it looks placid enough. Olivia and I both comment that it looks just like Voldemort's cave in *Harry Potter and the Deathly Hallows.*

"Hey, Ty! Pull us over into that little cove and maybe we can get into that cave."

"Cool. That sounds fun."

My vague plan is to get a photo from inside the cave, looking out at the river, but Ty's response turns out to be proverbial "famous last words." As we approach the cave, the river that looks so calm pushes our starboard side against the wall immediately downstream and we are suddenly pinned there. Ty can only use one oar—the portside upstream one—and the "placid" waters are placid no longer. I look down in horror. Roaring up the side of the raft is an onslaught of water, pouring down all the way from Meagher County with plenty more where that came from. More accurately, the waters are pushing the side of our raft downward to the water's edge and we are mere moments from having it rush over the side, which will flip the weighted-down raft like a bath toy. We are going to capsize. Olivia and I are leaning toward the wall in a desperate effort to keep the raft level, but Ty keeps a cool head and does not panic.

With broad, deep, strong, one-armed strokes of an oar he is able to slide and rotate the raft along the wall until we are suddenly freed, spinning out into the main channel. It is a close brush with almost certain disaster. After catching our breath for a minute, we all vow that we will not underestimate the river again.

---

Wherever the shores of the Smith River are not solid canyon rock—that is, wherever there are shores at all—there is every shade of green. The beautiful, lush grass and reeds make perfect homes for a multitude of fowl. Families of Canada geese are making their home in this canyon this time of year, and the goslings still have their adorable adolescent look. Fathers and mothers herd their ganders in and out of the water. They seem to mix well with families of merganser ducks. Merganser males have curious spiky feathers on the tops of their heads, giving them a sort of rebellious look.

Perhaps they really are rebellious. We slowly pass by a tiny merganser chick screaming and frantically running on the water downstream. His lollygagging has left him behind—he is clearly the black chick of the family. Thirty or forty yards ahead we see the rest of the McCallister clan cruising downriver, blissfully unaware they've left Kevin "home alone." He doesn't seem to be gaining on them and as the river sweeps us out of sight we wonder if his absence will ever be noted. We count *thirteen* other chicks to keep track of, all of them wisely following close behind their parents. Poor Kevin.

Around mid-afternoon we round a sunny bend. So far the sky remains blue and there is no sign of the dreaded storm. On the left-hand shore three white Teepees appear. It is obviously some private encampment rather than a Forest Service boat camp, and Bill—some distance ahead of us—explains that this is the "ranch."

He means the famous Heaven on Earth Ranch, the fame of which extends at least to everyone who has ever rafted the Smith River. The ranch is a private retreat and vacation spot with cabins for rent, but for people traveling by boat through the wilderness canyon, it is a beloved midway supply station. People stop to replenish their supply of ice and other sundries, but more often just to visit the fully stocked bar.

As we pull into view, we are struck with the odd and completely discordant beauty of the place. We are in as remote a place as one can possibly get in the continental Unites States, yet spreading out before us are cabins, outbuildings, and a beautiful green 9-hole golf course! On the other side of the river immediately opposite looms a spectacular limestone cliff, bathed orange in the sunlight.

We swing our raft into the shore and tie up among numerous other vessels. It is strange finding civilization and a multitude of people milling about. Our first order of business is finding the outhouses, which turns out to be no trouble. We think about hanging around at this veritable oasis for awhile, but these thoughts are quickly dispelled when a mighty and angry roll of thunder comes echoing down the valley, bouncing directly off of the cliff in front of us. It is nice of the storm to announce its imminent arrival. We quickly get back to our raft and push off, eager to make our camp.

Just a few miles downstream we arrive at our scheduled encampment at Upper Trout Creek. I should explain "scheduled." With the number of parties launching every day, the Forest Service requires each one to pick a boat camp for every night at initial launch so that they can manage the number of people at each spot. In essence, our camp is reserved for this night, and we need not worry that others will contest it. As we pull off to the shore and tie up our raft, the clouds are dark and menacing. The thunder has not stopped since we departed the Heaven on Earth Ranch.

We quickly jump out and start grabbing dry bags and heaving them on to the grass on shore. Twenty-five yards away there is a small ridge, on top of which is a grove of mature evergreen trees—it looks like much desired shelter, and that is thankfully exactly where we find the fire pit and campsite. It takes us several trips to get everything up to the camp underneath the trees—I slip in the mud twice—and then we set to work getting our tent set up and arranged for the night. While Ty, Olivia, and I are arranging our things and Betty is busy setting up her and Bill's tent, Bill is tying a waterproof lean-to between two trees.

Just as Ty and I finish setting our coolers a good distance away with a battery-powered bear fence around them, the sky breaks and everything turns white. It is not rain. It is hail, among the largest any of us has ever seen. Each "droplet" is about a half-dollar in diameter, and is joined by thousands of others. It is deafening as it hits the river and the cliffs on either side. Ty and I race to the lean-to, getting beaned in the head a few times, and we crawl underneath it. Bill, Betty, and Olivia are already there. Ty exclaims: "What the *hail* we're we thinking!?" We weren't thinking; we were praying. And our prayers—no, I guess *my* prayer was answered. How else should I explain that this began *precisely* after we had finished preparing our camp? An accident or coincidence? That is what most people would say, but I don't believe in accidents or coincidences.

We glance out and the river is boiling with hail striking the water. The ice is piling up on the ground around us. The ledges of the cliff all down the canyon look like they've taken on a layer of snow. The next morning Olivia will find some baby fish lying dead near the shore, pummeled to death in the shallows by hail. During the lull that follows the hailstorm I make my way upriver in the darkening light and try out a dry fly on a pod of feeding trout. As soon as I return, the rain begins. Steady and hard it falls, and we are confined to cover for the foreseeable future.

Bill and Betty break out their camp stove, fueled by a marvelous artifact of human refining—white gas—and boil water for coffee or tea. Ty is not particularly hungry, so Olivia and I heat up a can of soup for dinner. The rain shows no signs of abating, nor is it supposed to until a day or so from now.

As Bill tugs on his 151, Ty and I break out our own supply of firewater. Amazingly enough, it is for the first time on our journey and it also happens to be the perfect time.

---

WE HAVE CHOSEN RIGHTLY. Yes, we have chosen according to my particular taste and experience, but, still, we have chosen rightly. It is the mighty Laphroaig (*lah-froig*), a single malt whisky from the small island of Islay off the southwest coast of Scotland.

I must take an excursus to sing its praises. My mother is half-Scottish, and I spent three years in our ancient homeland working on my doctoral degree. Fondly, I remember the days when my friend (and colleague) Christopher and I would catch a train from Aberdeen, on the northeast coast, down to Edinburgh to spend the day in the library at what they call "New College"—probably because the school was started as recently as the mid-19th century, whereas ours dates back to 1495. Aberdeen's "Queen Mother Library" really was a bust in those days for my research interests and all the good books were at New College. It was worth the trip, in other words, for research purposes. As result of these ventures, however, I often joke to people that I worked on a "side thesis" in Scotland: "The Affects of Single Malt Whisky on Human Physiology." It took a lot of "empirical research," if you catch my drift.

Christopher and I would finish at the library late afternoon, and then head up and just around the bend to the Royal Mile. Edinburgh Castle gleamed in the twilight immediately on the right, and straight ahead was the "Scotch Whisky Heritage Center" with its warm, welcoming lights. In the basement of the Heritage Center was, we knew, a bar. And inside that bar was a bottle of basically every single Scotch whisky ever distilled.

Put another way, "Heaven on Earth" is not actually a ranch with a 9-hole golf course in remote central Montana. It is on the Royal Mile just below the castle in Edinburgh, Scotland.

Christopher and I learned much from this and other distillery adventures. We learned that Scotch whisky is spelled, "w-h-i-s-k-y," with no "e." Canadian, American bourbon, and other like beverages are all spelled with an "e." Unlike *Anne of Green Gables*, an "e" in this instance makes the thing less interesting. We learned that the noble Celts north of Hadrian's Wall are capable of distilling an endlessly diverse variety of beverages from the ingredients of barley and water, and nothing else. Nobody else anywhere in the world seems capable of this (Japanese whisky is a novelty, but—much like their baseball—it is nowhere close to the Major Leagues), which helps explain why Scotch whisky is routinely one of the top-selling spirits in the world. But think of that: this tiny nation, not much larger than the surrounding *counties* I am in, produces and sells enough of their national spirit to compete with...*vodka*? No offense, but Vodka is tasteless global moonshine anyone anywhere can make, out of any pile of garbage they have lying around—potatoes, corn, and such—and they do.

In reality some Scotch distillers use one other thing besides barley and water, but not in the way you might think. Lots of spirit-makers in the world use additives to spice up their otherwise nondescript flavor (e.g., apple, cinnamon—yay, Fireball!— orange, etc.), but this ingredient does not qualify as an "additive."

They use peat. Mud, essentially.

The island of Islay has one unique natural resource, and it happens to be the very thing on which the islanders stand: peat bogs. They slice giant rectangular chunks of the peat underneath their feet and dry them. In the rather ordinary process of drying the barley for their malting, they pass a conveyor belt filled with germinated barley directly over a peat fire, and the amount of smoky flavor passed on to the final distilled product will amaze you. Or it might disgust you; it is very much an acquired taste. Laphroaig is an island distillery that has over the past two hundred years mastered this technique, along with others like Ardbeg and—the crown prince of whisky—Lagavulin. Mostly because I cannot afford Lagavulin, the much more thrifty Laphroaig is my favorite, but trust me that I'm not missing too much in the way of quality. I call Laphroaig my "campfire in a bottle."

---

It is a campfire in a bottle on this night. The temperature drops, the freezing rain falls, and we are without a fire of our own. The warm peat and the soft, sweet of the whisky warms our chests and our spirits. We are overcome with gratefulness to God and love for each other.

Didn't Jesus call that the "summary" of God's law? Yes,

he did. Love for God, and love for others. In close concert with the Spirit of God, that is what the hearty, bearded Scottish distillers of spirit—these magnificent *sub-creators* —have achieved this night half a world away in the remote mountains of Montana.

The three of us are in our tent. The storm rages outside, and I say aloud my thanks for the answered prayer today, and then I give my boldest prayer yet: "Lord, you command the wind and the waves; we know that this storm is scheduled to continue all the way through tomorrow. Please let us wake tomorrow to clear skies. Blow the storm all the way through while we sleep. Amen."

Ty is quickly snoring, no doubt worn out from a day at the oars. I take my last sip of Laphroaig, kiss and say goodnight to my sweet Olivia, and curl into my dry and warm sleeping bag. I keep the flashlight on for a few minutes and jot down notes in my journal. With torrential rains thrashing down on our tent, I make a few silent prayers:

God, bless Ty.

God, bless Olivia.

God, bless my girls at home.

God, bless Bill and Betty.

And, God, bless all the crews busy digging peat and distilling barley on Islay.

## 7

# HIGH WATER & HORNETS

"Let us not be ashamed to take pious delight in the works of God open and manifest in this most beautiful theater. For, as I have elsewhere said, although it is not the chief evidence for faith, yet it is the first evidence in the order of nature, to be mindful that wherever we cast our eyes, all things they meet are works of God, and at the same time to ponder with pious meditation to what end God created them."

— John Calvin, Institutes

Floating along on the seam between half-dream and reality, I vaguely realize that it is cold. I instinctively burrow deeper inside my sleeping bag. I hear the pitter patter of water droplets on the tent, which tells me the rain has not stopped. A battle begins.

My sleeping bag feels like a geothermal hotspot.

Outside of my sleeping bag, it is freezing.

Inside my sleeping bag my body aches, sore from lying down on the ground for so long.

Outside of my sleeping bag, it is freezing.

Funnily enough, this is the exact same battle I fight every single morning at home, too. As often as I wish to stay in bed for the rest of my life—honestly, sometimes that seems downright reasonable—getting up always wins. Eventually.

I unzip the tent to retrieve my muddy boots that are tucked underneath the rain fly by the entrance, and everything is damp and cold. Ty and Bill have been up for some time already and they have managed to start a small fire, or at least what you would describe as a hot pile of smoke. I am mistaken: it is not raining. The water falling on the tent is moisture dripping from branches above. Miraculously, my prayer has been answered.

The storm has blown itself out.

The latrine at Upper Trout Creek is a hike, probably an eighth of a mile up a steep hill, and it is muddy this morning. There sits the toilet in a forest grove overlooking the campsite and river, but thankfully the Forest Service has built a sort of barrier blocking the view up the hill. On the other hand, the bears looking down on you from the other side have no such obstruction. I am kidding. There is no sign of wildlife at all, but it is quiet enough in the woods to feel creepy.

Later, as we stand close to the fire enjoying our customary Campstove Mocha, a sleek-looking canoe glides in to the shore. I spot the Forest Service logo on its side, and its lone occupant certainly maneuvers the vessel like an expert. The Ranger makes his way up to the camp. To my surprise, Bill hails him as he emerges up the rise. He responds, "Hi Bill!" As I've mentioned, Bill Black is a handy guy to have along.

The Ranger explains that he and a colleague in another canoe are leap-frogging down down the river checking on all the boat camps to make sure everybody made it through the storm in one piece. He had wisely stayed the night at Heaven on Earth, but he now plans to blast all the way out of the canyon today in advance of more inclement weather.

The weather continues to pose a problem for us, one we had discussed the night before. Our original plan had been to only float another ten or twelve miles to our next scheduled campsite. Given the weather, we really prefer to make more like seventeen miles, leaving us a shorter final day. This means we will have to make camp in an "unauthorized" location. For some reason, I am always nervous about breaking "rules."

---

Now this is funny. Truthfully, Montana is one of the "Last Best Places" in terms of not having lots of "rules." In the grand scheme of things, we are relatively free. Within very recent memory, not only did Montana not have speed limits on our highways and interstates, it was also perfectly legal to drink and drive (so long as you weren't impaired). And while the state manages the Smith River with a fairly heavy hand, what with its permits and rules and regulations, in most places, citizens have reasonably free rein when it comes to our public lands.

I was reminded of this when I returned home after spending three years abroad. In Scotland, one needed permission to do just about *anything*. And, of course, you generally had to pay handsomely for the permission—always on top of huge income tax rates and an added 17.5% Value Added Tax on literally anything you decided to buy. (Somehow the Scots still like to call their health-care system "free," though—something I always found kind of charming.) The relationship between citizen and state in the United Kingdom feels stifling, at least to a Montanan. The presumption is always that the state owns and runs everything, and you can enjoy things only by their leave. I once looked into fly fishing for a day at the Queen's residence at Balmoral Castle. Granted, that isn't public land, but I recall the permit cost a hundred pounds sterling—way beyond my means.

My friend Christopher came to visit me in Montana one October, fairly soon after returning to the States. I took him up the Beartooth Highway, which is only an hour from my house and easily the most beautiful highway in America. That's not just my opinion, either: that's a direct quote from famous travel reporter Charles Kuralt. We stood at the overlook viewing the jaw-dropping valley directly across from the Hellroaring Plateau (If you've ever seen a picture of a valley in the Swiss Alps, that's a good comparison). My eye caught a familiar thin, brown line cutting through a dense pine forest across the ridge on the far side. I had a wild idea.

We hopped back into my 2000 Mercury Mountaineer, my Montana "backroad beast," and headed back down the valley.

"Where are we going?"

"Just wait," I replied.

That thin brown line is the road that goes up the *other* side of the valley, all the way to the top of Hellroaring. And if the Beartooth Highway is the most beautiful road in America, around these parts the Hellroaring road is legendary for being the most *terrifying* in America. It is not a "highway" at all. It is a single-track, dirt-and-rock road without shoulders that regularly punctures tires. The vertical drop, in places just inches outside the car door, is hundreds of feet at the bottom and thousands at the top. Your stomach basically nestles into the region of your intestines for the duration of the drive.

At a slow crawl in full four-wheel drive, white-knuckled at every moment, we managed to drive all the way to the top, way above the timberline, and where we were finally plowing through deep snow. Along the way we met a group of people on four-wheel ATVs, and we barely managed to have enough space for us all to pass. They all said as they went by, "You guys are crazy." Crazy for attempting this drive, they meant.

The air was thin and cold. We stood at over ten thousand feet and could see all the way to the edge of the world. I asked Christopher: "Can you believe that we didn't need anyone's permission to drive up here?" He was equally incredulous. In the United Kingdom, a road like this would be barricaded and nobody would ever be allowed to drive it.

God bless the U.S.A.

---

FREE as we generally are around here to just up and drive a perilous mountain road with nobody's permission, I am still nervous about breaking "rules" when there are rules. And even if rules had nothing to do with it, I don't fancy arriving at a boat camp only to find it already occupied.

Bill isn't worried about this at all. He has already assured me repeatedly: "Nobody will be at Upper Givens." As usual, I'm not certain if it is actual knowledge, experience, or the 151 talking. But I know now that we are going to have to talk to the U.S. Forest Service Ranger about our plans to void our original "agreement," such as it is, to press further on down the river.

Sure enough: "What's your plan?" the Ranger inquires.

"We'll camp at Upper Givens," Bill replies matter-of-factly.

"Oh, good idea. Nobody will be at Upper Givens."

There is clearly some secret about this Upper Givens, and I am not in on it. And that gives me something new to worry about, now that I'm relieved of the guilt of making an unauthorized camp. We suddenly have the enthusiastic permission of the United States Forest Service to go right ahead and do it.

---

One glance at the river and I know why the tie-up posts for the rafts are placed so high on the shore. The water level has risen several feet overnight, and the river has decisively turned muddy brown. Our vessels are still secure, but there will be no more fishing for the duration of our journey.

Breaking down a camp is difficult and time-consuming work, especially after a night of rain. Everything seems damp and wet, and we take our time to let our tent and tarps dry off as much as possible. Inconveniences like wet gear make it so easy to forget the blessings, a truth that applies to all of life. But I am determined not to lose the plot. Every single forecast, every single scenario said that rain would continue throughout this entire day. I try to imagine breaking down our camp in a downpour, and am amazed that I have to imagine it.

Why is it not a reality?

My prayer has been answered. Of that, I am sure. Bill is not nearly as convinced, and continues to think the storm is sure to swirl around for another pass. That's one of the things I've come to notice about cynical people (not that Bill's a *complete* cynic): they can never seem to take yes for an answer. There's always a downside, some lurking unintended consequence, or—as I put it earlier—a dark lining in every silver cloud. Gifts are viewed with suspicion rather than gratitude. Some people go through life just waiting for the other shoe to drop.

The alternative is simple gratitude and thankfulness. It really is amazing that in the Bible when the Apostle Paul talks about humanity's deepest and most grievous sin, he doesn't jump to a laundry list of commandments that we disobey. Instead, he says we "neither glorified him as God nor gave thanks to him." What is our biggest problem? Thanklessness. Ingratitude. The inability to take yes for an answer, to simply receive God's blessings and acknowledge them as such.

Author Andrew Klavan wrote a moving testimony of how he converted to Christianity from his life-long atheism. One night he was reading a novel in which one of his favorite characters prayed before going to bed. He had a sudden thought: "Well, if he can pray, so can I." He laid the book aside and whispered a three-word prayer:

"Thank you, God."

Everything changed. He describes what happened the following day:

> There was a sudden clarity and brightness to familiar faces and objects; they were alive with meaning and with my own delight in them. I called this experience 'the joy of my joy,' and it came to me again whenever I prayed. Naturally I began to pray every day. And over time, this joy of my joy became a constant companion: a steady sense of vitality and beauty that endured even in periods of sorrow and pain.
>
> I was living in the beautiful Southern California town of Santa Barbara when I realized that prayer—that God—had transformed my life utterly, giving me a depth and pleasure of experience I had never known. I drove up into the hills one day, and with the forest and the city and the sea rolling by my windows, I asked God, 'How can I thank you for what you've done for me? What could I possibly offer you in return?'
>
> — Andrew Klavan, Christianity Today, August 22, 2016

That's how I want to live life, too—especially now, in

this moment, on this raft in this river. And I do see with clarity and brightness that my surroundings are “alive with meaning” and delight. This is all a gift. The only proper response is thankfulness.

I believe our culture’s overwhelming sense of depression is linked to ingratitude. I’m reminded of this when we spy three bald eagles over the course of the day. Everyone is familiar with these birds, but for most people their experience is limited to photographs. Pictures cannot do them justice. One is struck by their sheer majesty as they sit high above the river on branches, peering with keen optics into the depths. When bald eagles were placed on the endangered species list in 1966 there were 487 nesting pairs left (I have no idea how they arrive at such specific numbers), and this explains why I never saw them in my childhood. At the last count, there are now 9,789 nesting pairs in the United States, which explains why I now see them all the time. In fact, just last year I was looking out my living room picture window in my residential neighborhood and watched a bald eagle fly down my street, ten feet off the deck, with a freshly-caught bunny rabbit writhing in its talons.

I remember well the controversy in 2006 when the government proposed to remove the bald eagle from the endangered species list. I thought it was an occasion for gratitude and joy: we had collectively saved these glorious birds from extinction! CNN took a very different approach: a segment on the proposal was filled with ominous music and hand-wringing, with the narrator darkly suggesting that this spells nothing but doom for our national symbol! Here is the thing about so many "causes" and movements, whether political or environmental: we lose the ability to take yes for an answer. We cannot celebrate our successes or admire our progress—we just look for the dark linings, for the next crisis, for the other shoe to drop. Much of this is because activism quickly becomes an industry, and when money is flowing from doom-and-gloom predictions, it is best to keep those predictions coming. But it seems to me that ingratitude and cynicism is at its root, whether it is just fundraising for the cameras or whether it is real. Faking ingratitude is the same as plain old ingratitude.

On this day, I am so grateful to witness these creatures. For me, like for Andrew Klavan, everything seems "alive with meaning." It is as though God is putting on a continual performance of his splendor—no, not "as though." He *is*. We are the audience, and he directs his cast of characters (river, rocks, songbirds, geese, ducks, swallows, and eagles) to provoke in us delight, awe, and...thanks.

---

KLAVAN MENTIONED one more important thing: joy was his constant companion, "a steady sense of vitality and beauty *that endured even in periods of sorrow and pain.*" This is not the naïve worldview of Pollyanna where everything is wonderful even when it isn't. Sometimes there are dark linings and other shoes do, in fact, drop. The road we walk through life is filled with obstacles, challenges, and sometimes suffering. But the Christian knows that glory follows suffering, morning follows the night, the empty tomb follows the cross. In *all* things, including suffering, God works for our good, whether we see it clearly at the moment or not.

It turns out that Bill's cynicism is not entirely unjustified. Mid-afternoon arrives and a soft, yet energetic, rain begins to fall. God is literally raining on our floating parade. I could, of course, conclude that he simply wants us to experience being wet on our Smith River adventure —and I am wet, as I discover that my jacket is merely water *resistant*, not water*proof*. But in time I discover that God has something better in mind. In addition to watering me, along with all the flora and fauna and providing fresh water for the animals of the forest, he is setting the stage for a memorable sight.

We are rounding a bend in the river. The rain is softly falling, even though the clouds are breaking slightly, providing atmospherics of gold and amber. It is completely silent. On the far shore a lone Whitetail doe steps out from foliage into full view. She is magnificent. Her coat shimmers from the rain and diffuse sunlight. She is muscular and well-fed. She watches us warily, her head stock still. Suddenly, a fawn leaps out of the foliage and stands at its mother's side. Very few artists—certainly not Walt Disney—could ever come close to capturing this serene beauty. The fawn's spots are snow white against its burnt orange hide, and she (he?) too turns to watch us slowly pass by.

It is untouched beauty, but touched nonetheless by our gaze. And we are delighted to witness this maternal connection that usually admits no spectators.

And we are thankful.

---

IT TURNS out that the rain is not, as Bill had feared, the storm circling around for another punishing pass. It lasts only a half an hour, and soon we are following the *Boston Whaler* on the extreme left side of the river. I ask Ty why we're hugging the bank, and he now lets us in on the aforementioned secret to Upper Givens boat camp. It seems the bank has completely eroded where we are supposed to tie up our rafts. We are slowing down and hugging the bank so that we can literally grab the bushes and pull ourselves to shore. More importantly, the non-existent boat ramp is just on the near edge of a curve where the river takes a sharp downward plunge into one of its few legitimate rapids. If we fail to stop and tie up at precisely the right spot, we will be swept downriver through the whitewater and miss our camp altogether.

Thirty yards ahead Bill and Betty are literally grabbing the foliage on shore to stop themselves from the rush of water, and we are suddenly and quickly closing the gap. The water looks shallow enough, but it is swift. The trouble with being so close to the bank is that Ty cannot use both oars to slow us down. Just as we are about to collide with the *Whaler*, I make my exit from the raft. An exit that turns out to be slightly premature.

I leap into the water with the rope in my hand. I think I can gain solid footing by the shore and hold the raft steady. I quickly realize that I have miscalculated, as the water immediately sweeps me off my feet and I land flat on my back, the river rushing over me. I quickly stand, happily realizing that I *can*. It turns out that the water is shallow enough for me to hold my ground, as I had thought. I lost my balance because I was *moving* downstream when I hit the water.

I stand firm, holding the raft while Livie and Ty leap out onto the shore and tie the raft to the post. A successful landing, yes, but at the miserable cost of soaking the inside of my wading pants. I happily remember that I have exactly one more set of dry clothes stuffed in a bag somewhere.

---

We set off down a small, very overgrown trail into a small grove of trees where we find an equally overgrown campsite. I now understand everybody's certainty that "no one will be at Upper Givens." Nobody has maintained this site in a very long time, and it has probably been aeons since anyone camped here. I have this dramatically confirmed when, in the midst of setting up camp, I wander down the path to the latrine.

There I am met by an angry swarm of hornets.

So I make my way back to the camp as quickly as I left it, and inform the crew that we have a hornet problem at the latrine. As it happens, this really is a problem. One of our party has a health condition that makes the latrine a necessity, not a luxury. Ty sets off to investigate.

A minute later he returns and announces that, yes, there is a grapefruit-sized hornet nest *inside* the toilet. Good luck sitting on that. We ponder our options: just take some sticks and bravely go to battle with a vicious colony of hornets? No thanks. Try to spray our can of mosquito fogger on them? Likely not powerful enough to kill them on contact. At last, Ty suggests that we use the most potent and powerful force at our disposal: fire.*

* [Note: *What follows here may or may not be true. Let the reader be the judge. In these troubled times, I can easily imagine some bureaucrat at the National Forest Service reading this book—after all, it has "Smith River" in the title—and deciding to send me a $10,000 fine for, I don't know, vandalism or destruction of Federal property or something.*]

Ty carefully unscrews Bill's bottle of white gas—it is unlikely Bill will donate his 151, though that would probably work equally well—and pours some into a paper cup. Olivia is thrilled with this idea, and I want absolutely nothing to do with it. The two of them set off down the path. I cannot see what they are up to, but I can hear them well enough: whooping and hollering, and thankfully laughing. That is better than screaming in agony.

They capture their hijinks on video for later viewing. Ty tosses the white gas directly on to the hive, followed by a lit match. The nest, so painstakingly crafted by these murderous pests over the long months of campsite dormancy, looks like the Hindenberg. Fire engulfs it. Hornets bail out by the dozens. It falls from the inside of the lid and plummets down into the hole. Livie stands guard, blasting the survivors with the insect fogger. It turns out that this poison actually does work on hornets, and she spends a very jolly half hour doing a mop-up operation, hunting down the newly homeless and putting them out of our misery.

---

IT'S OUR LAST NIGHT, and we decide to keep dinner simple. Leftover mashed potatoes, tenderloin, a can of beef stew, and a spicy sausage contributed by Bill all goes into a single pot and it is delicious when paired with a glass—I mean paper cup—of red wine from a box. I don't think to ask Bill how well it pairs with Bacardi 151. That stuff has probably burned away all of his taste buds anyway.

I've changed into the last of my dry clothes, and have sufficiently warmed up from my swim in the river. And this is an unfortunate mistake. As soon as we finish eating, I take the empty pot down to the river to wash it out. Since there is no landing beach at Upper Givens, I have to kneel on the turf and reach down into the water below. As I am scrubbing I experience a strange sensation. My inner ear is already rocking gently from the imprint of floating on a raft all day, but suddenly the world is turning sideways. The entire embankment I am kneeling on breaks away and falls straight into the water, taking me with it. This is my second swim in the Smith River today, and my final set of dry clothes.

I am wet and cold, but the warmth of our tent this night mitigates the misery. I refer not to just the external temperature. Campfire in a bottle, a deck of cards, and joyful mirth warm the soul as well as the body.

8

# SHEEP OF HIS PASTURE

"He restores my soul."

— King David, Psalm 23

Our final day begins with a harrowing plunge into rapids as the Smith empties from its sharp canyon and the "slinky" begins to stretch. The hard edge of limestone walls against the sky softens and slowly gives way to green, rolling hills underneath the vast blue sky. Long-abandoned, weathered barns occasionally stand sentinel in the middle of boundless pastures. Flocks of sheep mill about on each shore, their sheepdogs visible keeping vigilant watch from higher ground.

This is the "boring" part of the Smith River, and travelers do seem in a hurry. Many times a raft cruises past us, its guide steadily rowing downstream—a hard-working Sherpa for the poor millionaire in the front still desperately and fruitlessly casting his fly into muddy soup, somehow hoping for an angling miracle. In this water, he will not catch anything even if his fly smacks a trout in the face. But perhaps the gentleman is simply bored with the new scenery and continues to fish because he lacks anything better to do.

When the only thing to look at is sheep in a pasture, we should probably study and reflect on, well, sheep in a pasture. That's what King David did in ancient days, as he sat keeping watch over his father's flock. He couldn't help but see metaphor and meaning in it. It is the theme of his most famous song, which is also arguably the most famous literary work of all time.

*A Psalm of David.*
*The Lord is my shepherd, I shall not be*
*in want.*
*He makes me lie down in green pastures, he*
*leads me beside quiet waters, he restores*
*my soul.*
*He guides me in paths of righteousness for his*
*name's sake.*
*Even though I walk through the valley of the*
*shadow of death, I will fear no evil, for you*
*are with me.*
*Your rod and your staff, they comfort me.*
*You prepare a table before me in the presence*

*of my enemies.*
*You anoint my head with oil; my cup*
*overflows.*
*Surely goodness and love will follow me all the*
*days of my life, and I will dwell in the*
*house of the* LORD *forever.*

— PSALM 23

Certainly, everyone knows that opening line! But the whole thing is full of familiarity. Is there a more versatile piece of verse? I can hardly remember a funeral where that hasn't been one of the readings. It is the screenwriter's go-to whenever a protagonist is in distress: "Even though I walk through the valley of the shadow of death, I will fear no evil." No other text in the Bible has spawned more artistic *kitsch* than Psalm 23—paintings, figurines, placards, and Internet memes. Its every clause is a ready-made nugget of wisdom to be deployed.

All this "quotability" is great for memorizing, but it has a downside: we can easily miss the point. Our temptation is to read the Psalm and start applying different parts of it directly to ourselves and our circumstances. When things are going well, when we feel well-fed and satisfied, we imagine ourselves in "green pastures beside quiet waters." When we are being humbled by life, we cling to another verse: "Your rod and your staff, they comfort me." When we face danger or distress, we talk of the "valley of the shadow of death" and resolve to "fear no evil, for you are with me."

Another approach is more typical of preachers: grab a metaphor, squeeze, and wring every ounce of juice out of it. "The LORD is my shepherd." Ah, yes. You see, we are sheep. By all means, let's talk about sheep! Skittish animals, aren't they? Easily frightened. Incredibly dimwitted, foolhardy, filthy, and utterly helpless. At this point the preacher is left with little to do because the applications write themselves.

What is almost always missed in these ways of reading is that this song is not a loose collection of aphorisms, fortune cookie promises, or nuggets of wisdom. When it came to songwriting, David was no Mumford & Sons, just stringing profound-sounding thoughts together. David's song is a ballad. That is to say, a *story*. He's describing a road trip, and we're invited along.

---

U2's lead singer Bono calls David the father of the blues (and he is), but we should also recognize a great balladeer when we see one. This one's a classic about "coming home." Whether it's country western's odes of truckers seeing blurry white lines on their way back into her arms, glam rockers sitting alone in hotels rooms dissipating themselves while longing for lasting love, or the bluesman wailing about how she changed the locks on the front door, songwriters always seem to find home just out of reach. This was true in ancient times, too. Around the same time David was writing about sheep in his pasture, across the sea a Greek poet was composing a truly epic variation on the theme: the one where Odysseus takes ten years to get home to Ithaca.

We all feel out of place, out of joint, and searching for a place of belonging. We're all looking for that place we are meant to be, where we're able to flourish as our very best selves, and to feel the blessedness and joy of being home. It's the stuff of all religion and philosophy. French existentialists like Sartre and Camus made "alienation" their great theme. Gurus, Gnostics, and Scientologists think that we are all castaways from some great realm of Nirvana. Thus, the modes, techniques, sex rituals, yoga positions, drug and diet plans all designed to get you back in touch with home. Others think home is wherever we decide to make it, so our task is to recreate this Nirvana on earth (utopia), usually through things like government programs. Not as sexy as the *Kama Sutra*, to be sure, but it has its millions of true believers.

These themes are everywhere because there's an element of truth in all of it. Children of Adam and Eve are "east of Eden," as Genesis describes it, cut off from Paradise, that place where Creator and creature dwell together in perfect harmony. There *is* something wrong. I saw as we drove past Hutterite colonies, sped up abandoned mining roads in Neihart, and floated all the way down the river these past few days how conflicted we humans are about our place in the world. We are hard-wired to make our mark, to steward and cultivate creation, but we are completely unsure of ourselves. So often we just make a complete mess of things. Something isn't working right. Humans and nature are an awkward fit, like forcing a hand into too small a glove. Genesis 3 puts it better: Adam and Eve will still have relative success cultivating the ground, but now there will be thorns and thistles and blood, sweat, and tears. We've lost Eden.

No wonder we long for home.

---

PSALM 23 IS something like David's own autobiography—only more. After all, he began his life in a sheep pasture, later spent time as an outlaw hiding in crags, valleys, crevices, and caves in the desert, and eventually ended up reigning as king. That happens to be the story of the Psalm: a lamb travels from green pastures through a dangerous valley and emerges a king.

It's a perfect three-act play, complete with a "Once Upon a Time" and "Happily Ever After," with a harrowing bit of narrative tension sandwiched in between. Act 1 opens in a peaceful pasture, but it doesn't stay there. Suddenly, in Act 2 the lamb is being guided along "paths of righteousness"—or "the right paths." He's leaving the pasture behind and going somewhere. That "somewhere" lies on the other side of a dark and dangerous place: the "valley of the shadow of death." Act 3 finds the lamb emerging from the valley, and the image changes to visions of royalty. A banquet is prepared, oil anoints his head (coronation), cups are overflowing, and the lamb finds a permanent home in God's house.

Exactly where the dramatic tension arrives is difficult to spot, mainly because translators have a difficult time figuring out what to do with the phrase, "He restores my soul." At first glance, it seems like a *feeling*, a kind of deep satisfaction or experience of being fulfilled, like one might describe the aftermath of a particularly lavish Thanksgiving dinner. But is it really describing the spiritual equivalent of a turkey-induced tryptophan slumber? In Hebrew the phrase literally reads, "He *returns to me* my soul." That's describing the Lord's *action*, not David's feelings.

Instead of understanding "He restores my soul" as a summary of the green pastures and quiet waters, let's try something different. Let's see it as a heading, a forecast, or foreshadowing of *what comes next*. The lamb is about to experience a harrowing journey through the "valley of the shadow of death" and this is a story of how the Lord "returns his soul to him." This is the plot of this particular road trip: how the lamb walks through death's shadow and comes out the other side *alive*. That's what "returns my soul to me" means: resurrection.

As a songwriter myself, I can assure you that most songs have at least one lyric that doesn't mean much to the audience, but means a great deal to its author: it can be just a word or two that hints at a meaning much deeper than the listener can detect. David includes one in this song, a phrase that nobody ever really stops to notice: "He guides me in paths of righteousness *for his name's sake.*" A VH1 "Behind the Music" documentary could no doubt sleuth out the meaning of that cryptic note, but since he's out of pop fashion we'll have to do it on our own.

David had an incredibly eventful life, from killing lions and bears in sheep pastures to slaying Goliath to living on the run with a small band of brothers. But there was one moment that outshined it all. It is recorded in 2 Samuel 7. One day God sent the prophet Nathan to give him a message. See if it sounds familiar:

> Now, then, tell my servant David, 'This is what the Lord Almighty says: I took you from the pasture and from following the flock to be ruler over my people Israel.'

That's already pretty much Psalm 23. Then God makes an extravagant promise:

> 'When your days are over and you rest with your fathers, I will raise up your offspring to succeed you, who will come from your own body, and I will establish his kingdom. He is the one who will build a house for my *Name*, and I will establish the throne of his kingdom forever. I will be his father, and he will be my son.'

David is overwhelmed that not only has God been faithful to him up to the present, but that he would promise his continued faithfulness into the future! David responds:

> And now, LORD God, keep forever the promise you have made concerning your servant and his house. Do as you promised, so that your *name* will be great forever. Then men will say, 'The LORD Almighty is God over Israel! And the house of your servant David will be established before you.

Here's a helpful hint about reading the Psalms and many Old Testament prophets: any time you find a passage that talks about "David," a "house," and a "name," it is talking about 2 Samuel 7. And this illumines that cryptic phrase in Psalm 23. A "name" is a reputation. People accused of wrongdoing always talk about clearing their "good name." When David talks of God doing something "for the sake of his *name*," he's talking about God keeping his promises, being the kind of God whose "word is his bond."

In other words, David is confident that he will be led on "right paths" and make it out of the "valley of the shadow of death" and one day "dwell in the house of the Lord forever" because *God will keep his promises to him.* No—a *specific* promise: David's descendant will be enthroned in God's house forever.

The song is not just an autobiography. It is a *prophecy*.

---

That's how the early Christians understood David's songs. David knew that he would die, but that God had nevertheless promised him an eternal dynasty. How is that possible? How can God make good on such a promise, when all face death? David reasoned that there is only one way God could do it, and he said so explicitly in another place (Psalm 16):

> Therefore my heart is glad and my tongue rejoices; my body also will rest secure, because you will not abandon me to the grave, nor will you let your Holy One see decay. You have made known to me the path of life; you will fill me with joy in your presence, with eternal pleasures at your right hand.

The Apostle Peter provides the interpretation in Acts chapter 2:

> Brothers, I can tell you confidently that the patriarch David died and was buried, and his tomb is here to this day. But he was a prophet and knew that God had promised him on oath that he would place one of his descendants on his throne. Seeing what was ahead, he spoke of the resurrection of the Christ, that he was not abandoned to the grave, nor did his body see decay.

How will God vindicate his Name? He will raise the dead.

---

WHO IS he that truly walked this journey?

Who is he that trusted his Shepherd to provide, not only in green pastures but in a wilderness?

Who is he that walked not just through the valley of the *shadow* of death, but death itself?

Who is he that emerged from the grave?

Who is he that is exalted over his enemies in victory?

Who is now the anointed king?

Whose cup of blessing overflows to the nations?

Who now dwells in the house of the LORD?

Who sits at God's right hand, with eternal pleasures forevermore?

It is David's Son.

He tasted death that we might live.

He felt abandonment so that we might know "you are with me."

He emerged from the valley so that we might share at his victory banquet.

He was exalted so that we might dwell in the house of the Lord forever.

The Lamb went to his death, and came out a king.

---

In the death and resurrection of Jesus, the great fracture that cast us "east of Eden" is mended, and things can now be as they were intended. Our relationship with God is restored, but so also our relationships with each other and to the rest of creation. Belonging to Jesus means no longer feeling like an alienated castaway, but rather a son and daughter whose rightful home is in God's house forever.

Having carved our way through dark canyons, now floating by green pastures and quiet waters, Ty, Livie, and I are headed home. We'll even be given one last reminder of our real and lasting home when we get to the place where all floaters leave the Smith River:

It's called *Eden Bridge*.

Someday we'll cross the real thing because Jesus led the way. And we will enjoy Him forever.

## ABOUT THE AUTHOR

Brian Mattson is theologian, writer, and musician. He lives with his family in Billings, Montana.

www.drbrianmattson.com

facebook.com/dr-brian-g-mattson

twitter.com/BrianGMattson

Made in the USA
Middletown, DE
21 February 2023

25307823R00078